America's Broken Promise

America's Broken Promise

Bridging the Community College Achievement Gap

EDUARDO MARTÍ

Foreword by John Ebersole

HUDSON WHITMAN
EXCELSIOR COLLEGE PRESS

Hudson Whitman Excelsior College Press
7 Columbia Circle
Albany, NY 12203
hudsonwhitman.com

The views expressed in this collection are those of the author
and do not necessarily reflect the views of the publisher
or any other agency, program, or organization.

Cover design: Phil Pascuzzo
Interior Design: Sue Morreale

Print ISBN: 978-1-944079-05-5
LCCN: 2016932621

This book is dedicated to
Patricia, Julie, Emily, Jason, Jelani, Laila, Ruby and Rose.

~

Contents

Acknowledgments

This book emanated from a compilation of my experiences as a community college faculty member, administrator and eventually president of three community colleges, Vice Chancellor for Community Colleges at the City University of New York and, lastly, as interim president of Bronx Community Colleges. Along my long career many have influenced and molded my thinking. From Joshua Smith, who as president of Borough of Manhattan Community College saved my administrative career, to Georgia McNeil, the Chair of the Board at my first presidency, who guided me as a young and inexperienced president, to Matthew Goldstein, who gave me the opportunity to lead Queensborough Community College and allowed me to witness first hand how one can transform a system, to James B. Milliken, who pulled me out of retirement to lead Bronx Community College, giving me the opportunity to capstone my career in a place that represents all the vicissitude that community colleges endure.

However, the students whom I taught and worked with were my best teachers. Listening to their needs, trying to help them meet their goals, and respecting their efforts to seek a better future for themselves is an impetus that cannot be ignored. It is my hope that this book helps future administrators and stakeholders to better the lot of the countless students who need our help.

Also, I want to thank, my friend and colleague, John Ebersole, who believed in this project and who was instrumental in bringing it to completion. Ms. Molly Gage, whose superb writing ability enabled me to polish my ideas and mold my words so as to make this a more readable work. And, thanks to Sue Petrie, publisher, who guided this project through its development.

Last but not least, to the person who inspired me throughout my career, Patricia, my wife. Without her support I would have not taken the chances that enabled me to do the things that I have done.

Foreword

John Ebersole

America's Broken Promise is not for those seeking further evidence of poor performance by our nation's 1,136 community colleges. It *is* for those who want a detailed explanation of the nuanced complexities that often place community colleges at odds with themselves. This book is neither hypercritical nor pollyannaish. And Dr. Eduardo Martí asks for no quarter by those who would hold him and his fellow CEOs even more accountable for results. Instead, he points to the actions and resources needed to meet the many expectations of the unique collection of critics surrounding community colleges.

With this book, Dr. Martí offers those of us who care about community colleges a complex portrait of these institutions—now serving more than half of America's 21 million college enrollees. And, he offers far more than a provocative title.

Dr. Martí's narrative follows the evolution of the community college as a bridge between secondary and tertiary education, and correctly sees its impact on both individual and community well-being and economic opportunity. He speaks passionately and at length about "the promise" [of access] that is implied by our society as community colleges are positioned to serve as a starting point for all with a high school diploma or GED, regardless of college-readiness or the ability to pay (thanks to Pell Grants).

Readers should especially appreciate his thoughtful analysis of the problems created by open admission that are enhanced, often unrealistically, by the expectations that accompany. Having dealt with unready, unrealistic, and often, unhappy students himself, Martí provides a heartbreaking picture of what happens when good intent alone runs aground on the economics of higher education today.

As a fan of John Dewey, Martí sets forth his own beliefs in the importance of community colleges: ". . . blending pots [for assimilation] for New Americans," helping immigrants learn a new language and lexicon, as well as an understanding of democracy as a system of national governance. Dr. Martí was a refugee from Castro's Cuba, and knows firsthand the importance of the schools of and for democracy.

In the second half of his work, Dr. Martí engages directly with the politically sensitive issues of community college achievement (the "Broken" part of the promise), and graduation.

Long criticized for their poor graduation rates by politicians, tax payer groups, and fellow educators, Eduardo points out that over half of those entering the community college's "open door" are not college ready and will require various forms of remediation. Additionally, he acquaints the lay reader to the "all things to all people" philosophy that has long plagued community college leaders seeking to boost graduation rates among students not necessarily intending to graduate.

By some estimates only one-third of a typical community college's enrollment is made up of students seeking a degree. Many leave after sufficient exposure to a vocational subject to gain employment. Another third intend to complete their general education requirements for a bachelor's degree (typically with significant tuition savings), and then transfer to a four-year school (without concern for graduation or a degree). Thus, only a final third look upon the associate degree as an objective in itself. Yet, to not "graduate" *all* of these degree seekers is measured as failure.

Rather than criticize his fellow presidents or suggest that their institutions are underperforming (what some may have read into his title), Dr. Martí points to the realities of un- or underprepared students, and the differing expectations for the inexperienced and unfocused students with little clarity of purpose or motivation to succeed. These students will require a level of personalized attention few programs are staffed to provide.

In addition to outlining the consequences of a "broken promise" around academic achievement, he spells out ways by which institutions can come closer to fulfilling the achievement promise, by naming, facing, and resolving the institutional challenges which often get in the way.

Introduction

Almost 50 years ago, I entered the complicated world of community colleges with little intention of staying in the field. I was trained as a biology researcher and had no interest whatsoever in pedagogy. The teaching job I received at Borough of Manhattan Community College gave me a way to feed my small children, but I saw it as a mere opportunity, a steppingstone to what I considered a "real job" at a "real university."

But something unexpected happened along the way.

The year was 1966. Lyndon Johnson's Great Society legislation was opening doors previously shut tight to ethnic minorities and women. The City University of New York was beginning to establish an open admissions policy whereby all students with a high school diploma were accepted regardless of their academic performance in high school. Suddenly, every high school graduate found a place to study among the colleges of the City University. The most underprivileged and sometimes the most underprepared found a place in the system's community colleges. The open admissions policy at CUNY appealed to my deep sense of social justice. The only requirement of students was a willingness to learn.

As the open door policy was put into effect, the colleges were thrown into an entirely new sphere. There was chaotic growth in

enrollment, and a need to rapidly change the curriculum to adapt
to new populations; numerous debates ensued about how to maintain standards while facing the influx of underprepared students,
and vigorous disagreements took place about developmental education and remedial education. The problem of how to provide high
quality, robust education to the underprepared was, and continues
to be, a challenge of enormous complexity. The new avenues open
for study and knowledge formation were intoxicating to a young
researcher. I may have started my community college tenure as a
dubious teacher, but I quickly became a convert.

My love affair with the mission of community colleges sustained me through 12 years of teaching and 28 years as a community college president. Now, with the clarity of vision provided
by the wisdom of age, I offer the words in this book to a new
generation of teachers and administrators. We must find ways to
ensure that community college students enjoy the opportunity of
access to higher education, but we also need to make every effort
to ensure that our students succeed.

I believe this quest to be not only for the benefit of individual students but for the public good. In fact, I believe that
education is the basis of a functioning democracy. Our population must be better educated to become good citizens. Without
a solid understanding of historical context, without the ability to
think critically, without the ability to communicate effectively,
people can be manipulated, governments can cease to be responsive to the needs of those it represents, and demagogues can thrive.
Therefore, universal, high quality, effective education is a matter
of national importance. In addition, in our global economy, the
younger generations must prepare themselves to meet challenges
posed by a rapidly changing and interconnected workforce. A
high school education is just not enough. Our population must
be better trained so as to be both productive citizens and thoughtful workers.

∾

Community colleges have been called America's Colleges because our leaders, administrators, and teachers believe that opportunities are limited only by one's persistence. Although we hold that all students, given time and resources, can be educated, we have not always made good on fulfilling this egalitarian aim. Questions about our community colleges persist today: can our institutions deliver on our critical mission? Are we the very best schools to educate and train our population? Perhaps most importantly, are we raising expectations of a vulnerable population without a real possibility of providing a pathway to success?

According to the National Center for Education Statistics, we cannot answer any of these questions conclusively. In a report issued in May 2014, while 57 percent of students attending a public 4-year, degree-granting institution graduated in 6 years, only 20 percent of first-time full-time students pursuing an associate's degree or certificate at a public 2-year institution completed said degree in 3 years. (Kena et al., 2014). Notwithstanding the students (and their numbers are not nominal) who choose to attend a community college to take only one or two courses or who transfer out to a 4-year college before graduation, an 80 percent non-completion rate is universally unacceptable.

∾

This book takes a practitioner's view of community colleges and offers an informed opinion of what is necessary to transform our schools and fulfill the community college promise to provide our students a path to a better life. It explores the origins and evolution of community colleges. It explains how these institutions evolved from institutions created to fulfill the dreams of individuals to better themselves, to institutions needed by local communities to prepare an educated and well-trained workforce. It explores how community colleges shifted from junior colleges and finishing schools to first provide a bridge between high school and 4-year colleges, and to then provide a bridge between post-secondary school and professional work. It describes how these colleges became an important component of local economies and how they became attuned to business community needs.

The book also explores the role of the federal government in the development of these colleges. The federal government has, since 1947, been instrumental in developing the national network of low-cost, accessible, local 2-year colleges. The involvement is grounded in the federal government's designation of community colleges as the institutions where America's workforce is trained (and often retrained), where underprepared youth can find a way into productive employment without incurring a crushing debt, where poor and underprepared ethnic minorities can begin along the pathway to the middle class, and where all who seek a post-secondary education can find it. Today, the federal government is more involved than ever before in making our schools both accessible and affordable.

Additionally, this book explores the current public awareness of the community college sector and explains how renewed interest—often expressed by the federal government—has placed a bright spotlight on outcomes, sometimes overshadowing the promise of opportunities. Although the attention is generally welcome, it has revealed the harsh reality that community college performances are less than effective. The book delves into the root causes of the failure to make good on the colleges' institutional promise. Without apology, the book exposes the difficulties presented by the sector's lack of selectivity; it shows the complexity of teaching *all* students who depend on community colleges to access a postsecondary education; and it points to the severe lack of academic and student support services that make the colleges' job so difficult. Deep examination provides insight into why graduation rates are so low and why success rates are typically so dismal.

There are serious problems facing community colleges, and this book does not shy away from revealing them. But there are also many promising practices at community colleges, and this book leverages them to illustrate the various alternatives to improving student (and institutional) outcomes. To that end, this book addresses new and effective approaches to using pedagogy and student support services to improve completion and graduation rates. It shows how relying on a diverse funding stream, from both government and private philanthropy, for example, can provide stable funding for our schools. These approaches and the others that I explain here should be taken as evidence of the further evolution of community colleges. Our institutions are places where individual aspirations can be fulfilled, but they are also places that substantively contribute to the nation's well-being.

As a long-term practitioner, I believe that the future of community colleges is bright. Public awareness, businesses, and philanthropic organizations have begun to substantively concentrate their efforts on community colleges. I hope that this comprehensive attention will ultimately result in producing a new kind of institution—one that is squarely centered on student success; one that considers the failure of any student equivalent to an institutional failure; and one that sees itself as intricately connected to the needs of the local community. An educated population is our best defense for a functioning democracy and for a thriving economy. Our colleges will continue to play an important role to these ends.

I wrote this book in the hope that present and future practitioners will benefit from the mistakes that I've made and the successes that I've helped facilitate during my presidencies. I also wanted to write in a way that provides members of the public a plain language insight into the workings of these important institutions. Accordingly, in this book, I explore how I have transformed institutions from places where students are merely provided with opportunities, to places where students' aspirations are turned to success.

Chapter 1

The Perils of the Promise

The Early Years

Although the America's College Promise Act indicates that community colleges are more important to America's postsecondary education system than ever before, the institutions often underperform and underwhelm students'—and society's—expectations. Today's community college leaders, administrators, faculty members, and policymakers work incredibly hard, but they struggle to define effective missions, accurately identify the needs of students, and devise appropriate measures of achievement. Consequently, systematic solutions that can solve the institution's problems have yet to appear. Now that the Obama administration has deemed community colleges crucial to preparing America's global workforce, it is time to revisit, redefine, and reinforce the promise community colleges extend to their students and their communities.

Most community college leaders, administrators, faculty members, and policymakers take pride in knowing that community colleges are the *only* postsecondary institutions that promise to educate and prepare *all* interested Americans for future degrees and professions. The promise, however laudable, puts community colleges on the line: our schools must meet the needs of students with widely divergent academic abilities and professional goals, with an extraordinary array of social challenges, and with sometimes excruciating financial obstacles. Unsurprisingly, our schools too often fail.

As a 30-year veteran of community college administrative affairs, I know that we can only serve our students by mending our historic institutional promise. We must therefore develop the strategies that will enable us to *effectively* educate *all* students. To begin this work, we must establish a clear and candid accounting of the institution's crucial place in American education. We must accurately identify the stubborn problems that continue to hold back our schools. We must avoid the empty assurance of piecemeal approaches and partial solutions. Above all, we must develop experiential and competency-based models for learning and technology-enabled pedagogy that will equip community college students for educational and professional success.

I believe in the vitality—in fact, the primacy—of community colleges. I also believe that we, as leaders, administrators, faculty members, and policymakers, must adopt a more comprehensive, practical, and participatory approach to our institutional practices. Today we must work to consolidate our import and invigorate the promise that makes America's community colleges so vital.

∾

To redefine the expectations of what an American community college can and should be, we turn first to our students. Unlike other postsecondary institutions, our colleges are characterized by the hyperlocal needs of our communities. This necessary attention to locality means that community colleges not only differ from more traditional postsecondary schools but also differ, and sometimes radically, from other community colleges. When it comes to our institutions, there simply is no one-size-fits-all: a community college like Valencia in Orlando will tailor its offerings to students seeking professional skills in tourism and vacation-related industries; meanwhile, a college like Fort Peak in Montana responds to the needs of a large Native American population and students who care deeply about language and cultural preservation.

Devising solutions to teach and support diverse community college students is a complicated task. Yet the colleges often face the very same obstacles when working to meet student need. First, there are challenges associated with inadequate preparation. Public community colleges accept anyone with a high school degree, so classrooms are filled with students with dramatically different experiences and intellectual abilities. This creates a heterogeneous classroom environment that is made the more challenging by students who believe that community college is a step down from a "real" college (Cohen, Brawer, & Kisker, 2013). Such a perception is fueled by the too-general assumption that community colleges offer inferior educational and professional opportunities. It is also reinforced by a potentially pointless five-hour placement exam that determines incoming students' skills in writing, reading, and computational ability. A January 2014 report from the Community College Research Center revealed that as many as 68 percent of students routinely place in at least one remedial course.

Second, there are the challenges associated with scarce financial resources. To put it plainly, many community college students lack the funds to attend *any* postsecondary school. Without substantial monetary support, few incoming community college students will achieve the success they dream of and strive for. Further, because most community college students must pay for at least some remedial studies, they often begin their postsecondary education with a debt in preparation *and* a debt of dollars. Students will pay for remedial courses with federal and state financial aid, but doing so eats up money that would be far better spent on more advanced coursework.

At Bronx Community College (BCC), where I've served as interim president for the 2014–15 academic year, we boast low tuitions of less than $3000 per year. However, even despite the relatively small number, many of our students simply cannot afford to pay. In the fall 2015 semester alone, 1584 students had outstanding bills that prevented them from registering for the spring 2015 semester and completing the associate's degree in June. We were able to buoy 1000 students through private grants, but we just couldn't help the others. Over and over again, we find that these students—the ones who do not believe that they can achieve their goals and who cannot find enough material help to do so—give up their dreams of education.

Third, and probably most devastatingly, there are the challenges that are woven into the social fabric of our students' lives. I saw these difficulties myself nearly fifty years ago as a young biology instructor at the Borough of Manhattan Community College. At the time, I thought I was a pretty good teacher. These were the late sixties, way before the advent of experiential learning, cohort-based problem-solving methods, technology-aided instruction and other more contemporary pedagogical techniques. At that time, a good teacher was someone who could keep the students engaged, who could cover all the material in the syllabus, and who could provide well-crafted multiple choice questions that the majority of students answered correctly. Let me repeat, I thought I was a pretty good teacher.

Then I faced a situation in which I realized I just could not measure up to the need. "Adam," an African American student who was doing well in my course, stopped coming to class. When he reappeared, I asked him to stay and talk. I assumed that something was going on at home, a pretty common situation among my students. I asked Adam about his absences and lectured him about the importance of attending class. At first he was annoyed, but eventually he actually looked hurt by my tirade. Finally, he stopped me midsentence. After some awkward hesitation, he came out with it: he had to skip class because his traveling buddy was sick.

I don't like to admit it now, but at the time I almost laughed. What kind of excuse was this? Why would he skip class because of his buddy? Then he told me that he needed to go to school with a friend because going from Harlem into Manhattan meant going through "hostile" territory. When I suddenly realized what he meant, I also realized that his struggle for an education went way beyond trying to get good grades. For Adam, like for a lot of my students, it was a matter of life and death. Even though I actually *was* a good teacher, I never figured out how to help Adam. He simply stopped coming to class.

I wish I could say that things have changed for the better, but community college students still work to overcome so much. A recent student at Bronx Community College provided a stark reminder of the radical student need our institutions strive, but often fail, to meet. Kalief Browder came to Bronx after being held at Rikers Island for three years without bail. Although charges were dropped and Kalief was eventually released, he was obviously deeply scarred from his experience. At BCC, he struggled to find his footing. But he worked hard and gained his high school equivalency diploma in Future Now, a BCC program for formerly incarcerated students. By the spring of 2015, Kalief had declared a liberal arts major and boasted a GPA of 3.562. Unfortunately, but probably unsurprisingly, Kalief's success was not enough to sustain him. He committed suicide in the summer of 2015. The BCC worked hard to meet Kalief's needs, but his life and premature death remind us that we have yet to provide a safety net with which to catch our most vulnerable students.

Students like Adam and Kalief, and administrations like Queensborough and Bronx Community College illustrate the simple fact that community college students are different. To reach these students, our institutions need to recognize that we serve a far more vulnerable population than is or even can be served at other postsecondary institutions. We must also recognize, and often over and over again, that as community college leaders, administrators, faculty members, and policymakers, we have to be sensitive to our students' education goals, but also to their sometimes desperate need to improve their financial and social situations.

∾

Our students' challenges help to outline the contours of the needs our institutions strive to meet, and the numbers support the illustration. The American Association of Community Colleges 2015 Fact Sheet tells us that in 2013, students seeking undergraduate education at community colleges made up 46 percent of all students seeking postsecondary education. The students differ markedly from students entering traditional 4-year schools: 72 percent are aid-seeking students, 62 percent are full-time students who also work full- or part-time, and 36 percent are the first generation in their families to attend college (AACC 2015 Fact Sheet). Beyond each student's personal hopes and dreams, their collective numbers indicate that the success of *these* students—students who seek but who cannot always find success in postsecondary school—is absolutely crucial to America's continued social and economic vitality.

∾

Of course, many at community colleges readily recognize the impossible position our institutions occupy. We must meet students' complicated needs, accommodate ever larger numbers of students (AACC, 2015), ensure competitively high curricular standards (Bailey, Jaggars, & Jenkins, 2015), provide evidence of materially improved retention rates, and spend fewer dollars to meet our goals. It is no wonder that community colleges fall short on delivering their educational promise (Abrum & Roksa, 2011; Bailey, Jaggars, & Jenkins, 2015). However, when community colleges fail, it reveals as much about the extremely complicated role of education in achieving some semblance of the American dream as it does about the institution.

The current federal administration appears to recognize this, too. In the 2015 State of the Union Address, President Obama argued that community colleges are at the frontlines in fighting for education equality and educating America's global workforce (Reed, 2013). To support the institution's import, President Obama envisions spending 60 billion dollars to make the first two years of community college "as free and universal in America as high school is today." The money would make community colleges more accessible and would help enact the American Graduation Initiative to produce 5 million more postsecondary graduates. The practical application of President Obama's proposal is impossible to predict, but the proposal shines a national light on both the contemporary struggle of community colleges and their undeniable importance. With their open-door admissions policies, unbelievably passionate teaching force, and incredibly dedicated administrators and leaders, community colleges continue to offer one of the last avenues whereby every student can theoretically achieve the financial security and well-being virtually promised by a good education and exposure to opportunity.

Thanks in part to the federal administration's attention, community colleges play a big part in the conversation about American postsecondary education. Theorists and practitioners who have long informed community college development have taken active notice. Walter Bumphus, George Boggs, Gail Mellow, Eduardo Padron, Thomas Bailey, Shanna Smith Jaggars, and Davis Jenkins, in particular, have continued to uncover new paths for community college infrastructure and curricula. The zeitgeist argues that the time is right—now—to investigate the historical context that has informed the institution's current challenges, to redefine the community college mission and its potential for positive change, to call attention to solutions, and most importantly, to reinforce the community college's vital work as a contributor to a global workforce and an instrument of democracy.

∾

The birth and development of community colleges are rather vividly reflected in the college's contemporary promise and problems. As is the case today, the idea of community colleges was underwritten by a call for broader access to education and opportunity. This call drew on John Dewey's belief in the necessity of participatory education to found and promote participatory democracy. According to Dewey's theories, limiting admittance to education limits social discourse and, in turn, limits possible engagement with and within society. Early community colleges were built in part on the belief that access constituted an aspirational democratic promise.

While the appeal to access catapulted the community college to an important place in American education, it also deepened institutional responsibility and accountability for student achievement. Most education historians are well aware that the demands associated with both the necessity and desirability to educate more, and more kinds of, students created many of the difficulties that persist today. I believe, and I am hardly alone (Bailey, Jaggars, & Jenkins, 2015; Bensimon, 2007; Dowd & Tong, 2007), that the wide gap between access and achievement is the most intransigent problem facing community colleges today. However, the tension is not only as old as the community college's first iteration, it serves in important ways as the engine by which community colleges continue to develop.

∾

Looking back, we can see the many ways in which the tension gained traction. The schools that paved the way to later community colleges took root in the popular foment for education that began in America in the mid-nineteenth century and took a wide hold in the late 1890s. Previously, America did not possess any conceivable *system* of higher education; instead, it mostly possessed the disparate colleges that were founded in the late seventeenth century to serve the uniform cohort of white, wealthy, male elite (Brint & Karabel, 1989). When in the mid-to-late nineteenth century a collective desire galvanized for a broader education base, a more formalized system began to be imagined (Veysey, 1965). The motivation was prompted in part by a "turning point" in the 1890s, when general society began to believe that a degree in higher education could signal specialized preparation and function as a sought-after commodity in the bourgeoning American marketplace (Veysey, 1965, p. 264).

The demand called for a more comprehensive effort toward institutional development, and the beginnings of development helped to fuel the demand. Although community colleges were not yet identifiable in this system's initial—and initially haphazard—form, the schools that helped to cast the model for the more democratic, more socially egalitarian, and more socially engaged agenda that would come to characterize later community colleges began to proliferate after the passage of the Morrill Acts.

The Morrill Act of 1862 is usually situated as a watershed in the development of public education. It *was* a landmark, and especially on the road leading to community colleges. After all, it signaled one of the first major instances of federal aid intervention in higher education. Perhaps more importantly, it nodded toward the democratic impetus behind higher education's expansion (Thelin, 2011). The legislation was pushed by Vermont Senator Justin Morrill, gained traction during the Civil War, and was signed by Abraham Lincoln in July of 1862. By gifting 30,000 acres of federal land to each state to sell in order to finance the development of institutions devoted to "agriculture and the mechanic arts," the first Morrill Act reflected a substantive national desire and need for a more comprehensive, more *accessible* system of higher education (Hilgard, 1882; Land-Grant College Act, 1862). The second Morrill Act passed in 1890. It targeted former Confederate states and sought to make institutions similarly focused on agriculture and mechanics available to African Americans and former slaves.

The acts set a stage on which a system of higher education, and later, a system of community colleges, could play out. Ideally, by providing more access for more students, such a system would encourage the formation of institutions and student populations that markedly and meaningfully differed from the exclusively white, wealthy, male elite educated at America's earliest colleges (Diener, 1986). While the first Morrill Act cannot be reasonably considered to have come close to opening higher education to all American families, the act succeeded in laying out both the plans and the rhetoric by which a more egalitarian mission of American higher education could be sketched.

The acts brought about other changes, as well. For example, the acts helped set a different tone for higher education classrooms. Early American classrooms often overwhelmingly (and unsurprisingly, given early Americans' pedigrees) relied on a conservative European and particularly English pedagogical approach (Brubacher & Rudy, 1958), as was recapitulated at Harvard and the College of William and Mary. The style was grounded not in knowledge production but in knowledge transmission (Diener, 1986). When classrooms began to diversify, faculty members began to opt out of the traditional, classically oriented curricula and teaching styles and embrace a more practical, mechanical, and ultimately vocational focus (Diener, 1986).

The acts also helped to more firmly embed the theme of democratization into America's educational institutions (Vaughan, 1986). This was the result of the first act's intent and its language. The latter explicitly articulated the promotion of "the liberal and practical education of the industrial classes in the several pursuits and professions of life" (Land-Grant College Act, 1862). Its words reflected a desire to construct a system of education that emphasized upward mobility in America's otherwise rigidly stratified society. This is the reason for the symbolic and some-times-aggrandized role the acts play in conversations about the systematization of American higher education (Thelin, 2011).

A note on this overstated symbolism: despite general claims to the contrary (claims usually resting on a belief that early immigrants to America's shores equally benefited from democratic ideologies), social plasticity was not underwritten in early America (Thernstrom, 1964). It was certainly and emphatically *not* underwritten at the earliest American colleges, which educated a very particular group of men. The Morrill Acts worked to situate education, and specifically higher education (Ratcliff, 1994), as a tool by which an American dream of a more practically democratic, upwardly mobile sort could be conceived. The opportunity offered by the promise of wider access to higher education (and the related promise of a far more expansive common-school education) was at least initially a hard-won testament to the growing national belief in equitable attainment and an important contributor to the conception of the American dream (Brint & Karabel, 1989).

Of course, neither the first nor second Morrill Act resulted in a sudden outbreak in construction of universities, colleges, or community colleges. The acts did not prompt the more explicitly democratic-minded and community-based educational agenda that characterized later community colleges. The acts merely helped to invite a larger chunk of the American population to participate in the possibilities of higher education's still relatively obscure promise. In this capacity, the acts serve as an ideal frame through which to view the growing belief during the late nineteenth century that education could serve as a meaningful and potentially desirable avenue to American participatory adulthood. They can also be seen as helping to drive the momentum for the educational infrastructure that would be more meaningfully constructed at the turn of the twentieth century and beyond.

By the turn of the twentieth century, Americans collectively placed a much greater emphasis on accessing education in general and on accessing higher education in particular (Brint & Karabel, 1989). The numbers of students seeking higher education reflect the growing aspiration: according to Ratcliff (1994), at the beginning of the century, 4 percent of American young people sought higher education; by the end of the 1920s, the percentage had risen to 12 percent. It followed that more interest resulted in a jump in increasingly diverse students. Although still certainly "remarkably homogenous" by today's standards (Veysey, 1965, p. 271), the students seeking higher education began to consist not just of the white, wealthy, male classes, and not just of the Morrill Act's industrial classes, but also of the women who started their search for an educative home in higher education, and—although far less often—of the immigrants who sought refuge on American shores and the former slaves and their descendants who sought an education equal to whites (Veysey, 1965, p. 271).

The consistent inflow of new and (moderately) different students, more than any particular external force, mandated the institutional expansion that left a permanent mark on America's nascent education system. Consequent to increasing interest and increasing enrollees, tertiary institutions in particular began to grow and proliferate at a faster and more far-reaching pace than secondary education (Ratcliff, 1994). The counterintuitive development laid the foundation for structural reactivity. In fact, the characterization of the American system of education as vulnerably *reactive* rather than advantageously *proactive* persists today, and for good reason (Ratcliff, 1987). The task of preparing students for the rigors of higher education fell (and still often falls) most heavily—and most inefficiently—on the shoulders of the higher education institutions themselves. It was and is the responsibility of these institutions to provide remedial courses for unprepared students, to develop standards necessary for success, and to communicate those standards to secondary schools (Ratcliff, 1994).

Consequent to this inefficient alignment, a gap opened up that substantively separated secondary and tertiary levels of education (Brubacher & Rudy, 1958). The gap also constituted an opportunity; one that the relatively new institution of the proto-community college could bridge and fill. We might argue that the unsteady and irregular beginnings of the broader standardization and systematization of American education made just such an institution necessary (Cohen, 2001).

From the start, community colleges were totally unlike private and land-grant institutions. The latter two institution types found it necessary, although not necessarily ideal, to reach back to secondary schools to better define the success of their own institutions. The former were originally perceived and created as *already* placing one foot in secondary education and one foot in higher education. Unlike more traditional institutions, the institutions that would set the standard for today's community colleges were, in idea if not in practice, both proactive and connective.

~

All educational institutions in the early twentieth century—from junior high schools to high schools to early community colleges to colleges and universities—operated in a state of flux. Early community colleges were junior colleges (Vaughan, 1986) and were especially fluid, in part because of the intermediary role they sought to serve (Beach, 2011; Brint & Karabel, 1989). Junior colleges developed in tandem with junior high schools, also "conceptualized and initiated" during this time period (Beach, 2011, p. 6). But junior colleges and junior high schools shared more in common than an adjective. The two institutions were structurally and conceptually connected: both were usually housed in high schools or on high school campuses (Koos, 1924), and both were originally conceived as steppingstones to high school or college.

Consequently, junior colleges operated in a connective capacity, reaching out from the public-school system (Beach, 2011; Eells, 1931; Koos, 1924) toward the baccalaureate degree. Leonard Koos (1924), a classic junior college researcher, famously described this divisive-yet-connective role as "isthmian" (p. 16). Junior colleges, wrote Koos, connected "the mainland of elementary and secondary education with the peninsula of professional and advanced academic training" (p. 16). Today, a better term might be "liminal." Indicative of a literal threshold, the liminal status of junior colleges *should* have allowed the institution to act as a doorway through which students could exit secondary school and enter more traditional, more rigorous institutions of higher education. Junior colleges were thereby conceived as *both* an extension of secondary schooling *and* an anteroom for more traditional higher education schooling. They were an endpoint *and* a possible pathway to traditional 4-year institutions and degrees.

The flexibility built into their beginnings ensured that junior colleges could offer an entrance through which students could access various educational opportunities. However, in practice, the flexibility was a liability. The institution's doubled focus not only called into question its organizational identity, it aligned the institution more convincingly with secondary schools than with traditional 4-year institutions. In many ways, the alignment was purposeful. Junior colleges' early advocates and first architects, men like Henry P. Tappen, Alexis Lange, and William Rainey Harper, imagined a German approach to American higher education. In their view, junior colleges served as insulating institutions that protected the traditional university's "emphasis on scholarship, faculty specialization, and research" (Diener, 1986, p. 4). Analogous to secondary schools and positioned as "upward extensions" (Koos, 1924, p. 5), junior colleges provided an educational path that offset the pressure on universities to provide for the unprepared.

While the position advocated by men like Tappen, Lange, and Harper emphasized access, it emphasized the inferior nature of that access. Lange of the University of California–Berkeley and Harper of the University of Chicago developed junior colleges as important contributors to secondary and tertiary education, but both men viewed junior colleges as more intimately connected with secondary schools. Lange, for example, supported terminal programs and technical subjects and wanted junior colleges to function as the 13th and 14th grades of a high school education. The purpose of a junior college in his view was to act as the "continuation and culmination of secondary education" (Lange,1917). It should not be occupied with the higher-education goals of more aspirational entrants: "the junior college will function adequately only if its first concern is with those *who will go no farther*, if it meets local needs efficiently, if it enables thousands and tens of thousands to round out their general education" (p. 471–72, emphasis added).

Harper, for his part, established a junior college at the University of Chicago, influenced Stephens College in Missouri, and established Joliet Junior College, the first and oldest community college, as an addition to a high school program in Illinois (Vaughan, 1982). He advocated and developed a similarly encompassing but similarly subordinate role for the junior college, describing its benefits as varied but as ultimately ancillary to what was offered at more traditional institutions. Junior colleges were to meet the needs of students who did not want to continue their studies; were to prompt students who would not otherwise do so to engage in some higher education work; were to enable professional schools to raise their standards; were to prompt high schools to raise *their* standards; and possibly most importantly, were to take the pressure off of institutions that did not possess the resources to educate students through the junior and senior years of higher education (Eells, 1931).

The early but firm association with secondary schools ensured that the attributes that made the junior college institution so ductile conferred on the institution a rigidly *subordinate* position in American higher education. After all, it is not easy or intuitive to understand how an institution, even a proactive one, can hold a close association with the secondary level of education *and* offer, compete or partner with the kind of education available at the tertiary level. The junior college's position spoke to its foundationally unique and ultimately riven role: born in the gap between secondary and higher education, the institutions were tasked with a contradictory duty to be all things to all potential students, a duty for which today's community colleges are still accountable.

∾

That junior colleges sought to educate a diverse student body to both go further *and* to "go no further," two clearly different and seemingly incompatible mandates, merely points to the earliest iteration of the tension between access and achievement that remains the contemporary community college's hallmark. From the critical perspective of sociologists Steven Brint and Jerome Karabel (1989), the tension is wholly negative. Brint and Karabel famously cite Burton Clark's watershed article (1960) to describe the junior college's inherent inability to fulfill both mandates—to provide access and facilitate achievement equally—as the junior college's "cooling-out" function.

While the institutions helped to shore up a national ethos about America as the land of opportunity, they simultaneously suggested that in this land opportunity is limited—both in terms of content and availability. That early junior colleges labored to educate students to both go further and to go no further, to privilege both transfer-oriented programs for interested, viable students, and capstone programs for secondary school, serves as apt illustration of the competing pressures that fostered all future development.

Perhaps surprisingly, not just *in spite of* these competing pressures and conceptual contradictions but *because* of them, junior colleges thrived. In the early years of the twentieth century, the schools carved out a crucial niche: unlike more traditional options, the institutions could offer students much more obvious continuity with secondary school, much wider access to elements of higher education, and the much more obvious benefit of locality. These core advantages made the colleges indispensible to the communities in which they operated, even in the early twentieth century. It was, after all, the junior colleges that met the needs of America's industrial boom after World War I, (Witt,

Wattenbarger, Gollattscheck, & Suppiger, 1994, p. 44). The ability to offer flexible educational opportunities ensured that the colleges experienced dramatic population and institutional growth. By 1930, Harper's Joliet Junior College, founded in 1901 and routinely recognized as the first junior college, was joined by 449 such institutions (Eells, 1931, p. 70).

~

The growth provided early justification for the institution. It also exacerbated its internal contradictions. The institution's hyperlocal focus, in particular, which contributed to its dramatic expansion, gave rise to an uneven and disconnected evolution (Beach, 2011). Junior colleges were able to answer to very particular regional needs, but doing so reinforced an institutional insularity that separated the colleges not only from traditional tertiary institutions but from other junior colleges, too.

In fact, the hyperlocality that characterized the earliest institutions (and that we still prize so highly today) obstructed the broader systematization of the junior college sector (Dougherty, 1994). The institutions did not have to rely on the interrelatedness or unification (usually prompted and promoted by regional associations) that characterized other tertiary institutions (Brubacher & Rudy, 1958). However, without the benefit of this kind of unification, junior colleges were hindered from developing a powerful voice about matters related to faculty, administration, students, accountability measures, funding, or anything else that impacted operation and growth.

This began to change in the 1920s, when the colleges gained an association, the American Association of Junior Colleges, now named the American Association of Community Colleges (Witt, Wattenbarger, Gollattscheck, & Suppiger, 1994). At this point in time, the institutions also gained more widely applicable accreditation standards by the American Council on Education (Eells, 1931). The AACC spoke specifically to the issues of the junior college's disjunction by providing a unifying description of organizational identity in 1922. According to the association:

> The junior college is an institution offering two years of instruction of strictly collegiate grade [. . .] that may [. . .] develop a different type of curriculum suited to the larger and ever-changing civic, social, religious, and vocational needs of the entire community in which the college is located (Eells, 1931, p. 162).

The definition provided by the AACC, and the emphasis on a "strictly college-grade education" reflected a growing desire to unwind the junior college's associations with secondary schools. Of course, even at this early date, the die had already been cast. Junior colleges were already viewed as subordinate to traditional institutions of higher education. The secondary status was a direct reflection of the institution's bifurcated mandate to educate students to both go no further *and* to go further. Although early on, the junior college claimed an "isthmian," "intermediary," and "transitional" function, its "second-class status" became more entrenched as the institution continued to expand (Zwerling, 1974).

The unifying focus provided by the AACC and its efforts to align curricular standards with collegiate-level work turned out to be the opening salvo in a battle that administrators, faculty members, and policymakers would fight on various fronts throughout the twentieth century. What enabled the earliest junior colleges to serve as a bridge—their liminal status, their implicit promise of wider access, their offer of continuity and locality—was a burden in comparison to more selective, more advanced, and more urbane traditional schools (Beach, 2011). During the Great Depression and beyond, junior colleges fulfilled Lange and Harper's vision by expanding dramatically to meet local need. But in so doing, the institution continued to mark out an ever more clearly inferior institutional position (Beach, 2011; Reed, 2013). As the sector grew, junior colleges only marginally competed or partnered with traditional institutions. They seemed relegated to merely "improv[ing] upon" higher education's "structures and efficiency" (Ratcliff, 1987, p. 151).

≈

Up to the 1950s, the position of the junior college as outside higher education became more entrenched. This was helped by a renewed focus on vocational and occupational training subsequent to the Great Depression. When huge numbers of unemployed workers sought relative refuge in educational institutions during and after the Great Depression, they landed in junior colleges (Dougherty, 1994). Traditional 4-year universities were out of geographic and economic reach for nearly everyone, but thanks to convenient locations and low tuitions, junior colleges were the most logical and most immediately responsive institutions. Junior colleges again met communities' deep needs, but this time, the institutions met that need through ongoing education and job training. Enrollment rates at traditional universities declined during this time period, but enrollment rates at junior colleges steadily increased (Witt, Wattenbarger, Gollattscheck, & Suppiger, 1994).

The junior college niche continued to expand, but because it depended on vocational and terminal curricula, it continued to be controversial. As temporarily unemployed workers gained entrance to community colleges, the transfer option that junior colleges also provided (which made the most obvious case for the institution's "collegiate-grade" status) became less popular (Witt,

Wattenbarger, Gollattscheck, & Suppiger, 1994). With every social crisis, junior colleges proved more vital to their communities, but that vitality began to be defined emphatically away from an ability to act as a conduit to traditional tertiary institutions. Instead, the junior college niche focused on its ability to provide continuing education and job preparation.

In place of the uncomfortable alignment with secondary schooling, junior colleges were more and more often aligned (and no more comfortably) with vocational and occupational training. Administrators who ensured that their colleges met their communities' needs found that the institution itself was more stubbornly relegated to that outsider niche. The Great Depression and the New Deal's state-specific inauguration of emergency junior college centers through the Federal Emergency Relief Administration helped to cement the position (Greenleaf, 1936).

Of course, the position was welcomed by some and eschewed by others. Walter Eells heralded the new focus (1931), calling junior colleges "the people's college" and describing them as full of "potential vigor and vitality" (p. 34). But the efforts of prominent AACC members like Eells and Koos to invest junior colleges with more vocational offerings were also considered dilutive, contributing to the persistently difficult alignment with traditional 4-year schools. The pushback was really nothing new: in fact, it repeated the pushback against junior colleges' association with secondary schools and reflected the old suspicion that the education conferred by junior colleges was inferior and "a subversion of equality of opportunity" compared to the education offered by more traditional 4-year institutions (Dougherty, 1994, p. 29–30).

However mixed this reception, the effort to integrate vocational and occupational elements into junior college curricula gained substantive support through federal measures, particularly after the results of the Commission of Seven report on California's expansive junior college system. Compiled by the

Carnegie Foundation, the report recommended a hierarchical rationalization for American tertiary education. Specifically, the report recommended that junior college administrators focus their efforts on the majority of students who would *not* transfer on to 4-year institutions rather than on the minority of students who would make the transfer. The report proposed that the majority of junior colleges should reorient their admissions processes and curriculum to reflect the increasing necessity of vocational training and terminal degrees (Brint & Karabel, 1989).

Up to this point, we have seen that the tensions that helped birth junior colleges in the early twentieth century also sustained and strengthened their development. The irony indicates that junior colleges *depended* on the competing mandates that defined them. Rather than solve its competing pressures—between secondary and tertiary schools, between vocational and transfer-oriented foci, between access and achievement—social crises like World War I, the Industrial Revolution, the Great Depression, and World War II solidified them. As the colleges occupied more federal and social attention in the latter half of the twentieth century, their vitality to the American system of education became even clearer.

During and after the 1950s, the competing tensions and pressures that defined junior colleges were enveloped by the G.I. Bill of Rights and the Truman Commission's Report, *Higher Education for American Democracy.* As a consequence, the institution of the junior college was endowed with a new name and was beholden to a federally approved legacy that continues to unfold in complicated ways today (Beach, 2011).

Like the Morrill Acts, the G.I. Bill of Rights plays an apparently outsized symbolic role in the development of junior colleges. The legislation was enacted in 1944 to provide an avenue on which to direct the influx of returning veterans, to serve as an expression of gratitude to servicemen for their mandatory sacrifice, and to thwart the economic stagnation that precipitated the Great Depression (Batten, 2011). In these capacities, the bill was an unbelievable success. When the term ended in 1956, it had served 7.8 million of the 16 million World War II veterans (U.S. Department of Veterans Affairs). The benefits it provided to veterans included stipends that covered tuition to institutions of higher education. The bill's easy and wide access to education transformed both the American system of higher education and the American way of life (Gilbert & Heller, 2013).

While the flood of veterans discharged by the G.I. Bill resulted in major changes for junior colleges, particularly in regards to their expansion and their legitimation in the higher education sphere, the education commission formed by President Truman outpaced the G.I. Bill's influence. The Truman Commission on Higher Education was formed to consider the G.I. Bill's impact on American higher education and to determine new directions for educational policies. Led by George F. Zook, who had helped to establish the AACC, the Truman Commission released its report in 1947 (Hutcheson, 2007). The report and its echoes marked a major epoch for junior colleges and for all American institutions of higher education. Its unprecedented recommendations ensured that the report's receipt was mostly mixed, but it succeeded in perhaps its most important goal: to establish at the federal level "a national rhetoric on higher education policy" (Gilbert & Heller, 2013, p. 417).

In an echo of the earliest junior-college mandate, the Truman Report's rhetoric overwhelmingly privileged an exhortation to access, and forcefully argued for the federal government's role in providing every interested potential student, regardless of "race, color, or creed," access to higher education (Farrell, 1949, p. 509). The report positioned the federal government as instrumental in helping to broaden the higher education playing field by making its institutions more affordable and for far more diverse participants (*Higher Education*, 1947). Its recommendations therefore required a previously unimaginable expansion of higher education.

The report's premise of equality was widely endorsed (Farrell, 1949), but the scope was controversial, especially given the unanswerable questions it raised about the breadth and depth of federal involvement in both public and private institutions (Brint & Karabel, 1989; Gilbert & Heller, 2013).

Much of the report's attention was directed at junior colleges as the means by which the report's recommendations could be enacted. It was not as "junior" colleges that the institutions could meet the report's goals, however, it was as *community* colleges (Gleazer, 1994). By dropping "junior," the report weighed in on issues of organizational identity, institutional affiliation, and practical focus. The report suggested that because the junior college no longer served as *primarily* a channel to 4-year institutions, it should be considered not in reference to its transfer function but in reference to its more modern function as a comprehensive center serving the many and varied needs of the wider local community (Brint & Karabel, 1989; Gilbert & Heller, 2013; *Higher Education*, 1947).

Thus, the report recommended that *community* colleges deepen their institutional commitment to access and consolidate their institutional commitment to vocationalism. Community colleges could then be defined as all-embracing institutions in which a community's occupational and educational needs served as the "primary reference point" (Gleazer, 1994, p. 19). The expansive definition required a corollary material expansion, and not just at the systemic level but at the level of individual schools. Only by envisioning a huge increase in courses, programs, and services could the Truman Report justify its move to make community colleges the future home to the majority of the number of students projected to receive higher education schooling (*Higher Education*, 1947). Notably, the report did not provide strategies or recommendations for funding or executing such an expansion, advocating instead for a tuition-free community college education that would be subsidized by local and state initiatives (Gilbert & Heller, 2013).

Not all of the report's recommendations were, or even could be, realized. For one, many recommendations were radical by the day's estimations. For another, and as indicated above, the logistical plans for implementation were lacking, and applicable sources of funding, especially at the federal level, were slow to emerge (Cohen, 2001). Despite this, the increase in students subsequent to the G.I. Bill and the attention extended to community colleges subsequent to the Truman Report brought forth a seismic mid-century shift for community colleges. Maybe the most meaningful impact of the report was not really in any direct or identifiable material change but in the rhetoric that positioned community colleges as a *linchpin* rather than a transitional uncertainty in American higher education.

All institutions were influenced by the report's emphasis on access and all subsequently partook in boom times. Higher education enrollment between 1900 and 1955 reflected enrollment growth of 29 percent: in 1900, 3 percent of students were enrolled in higher education institutions; in 1955, 32 percent of students were enrolled in higher education institutions (Beach, 2011). This growth was concentrated in the 1950s and 60s (Kim & Rury, 2007). By 1969, according to the NCES statistics (1993), "college enrollment was as large as 35 percent of the 18- to 24-year old population" (p. 74). The Carnegie Commission also emphasized the growth, reporting that higher education enrollments in 1969 more than doubled, reaching nearly 8 million by 1970 (Kim & Rury, 2007; Thelin, 2011), with community college enrollment accounting for approximately 2.1 million students (Thelin, 2011).

Some of that growth was attributable to returning veterans, but far more meaningful and more sustainable was the growth prompted by increasingly diverse students, including women, African Americans, Hispanics, other ethnic minorities, and wave after wave of postwar baby-boomers (Kim & Rury, 2007) who sought tertiary education in the wake of a federally mandated emphasis on *access*. Predictably, given the emphasis and the obvious spike after the Truman Report, growth in higher education enrollment was especially marked for community colleges. During the 1960s, community colleges began to open at a rate of 50 a year, with California, Florida, Illinois, Michigan, and North Carolina leading the way (Cohen, 2001).

In fact, community college enrollment jumped from 23 percent of all higher education students to almost 30 percent (Kim & Rury, 2007). But the lack of federal planning outside of the Truman Report's emphasis on providing wider access to more students meant that states had to pick up the federal government's slack in terms of planning and finances. Earlier efforts to provide broader unification for community colleges had not gained enough traction to impact the uneven evolution, and decades of little central planning at the local and state levels resulted in community colleges that "sprout[ed] haphazardly" to accommodate an ever-growing numbers of students (Beach, 2011, p. 22). The continued lack of national, statewide, or even uniform local standards for curriculum concerns, faculty and student guidelines, and funding criteria threatened to leave community colleges to the side as federal funding became available. As enrollments rose throughout the midcentury, standardization became a priority—a necessity to better connect the "divergent quality of different schools" (Beach

2011, p. 18) and to ensure that community colleges maintained a newly secure place on the higher education playing field.

States began in earnest the complicated process of actively planning for and facilitating community college growth. In this, they were influenced by the federal government's gradual but substantive gestures to fund the access to higher education described as mandatory by the Truman Report. The National Defense Education Act of 1958, which provided low-interest loans and debt cancellations for students who became faculty members (Thelin, 2011, p. 70), and President Lyndon Johnson's Higher Education Act of 1965, which provided the first need-based federal financial assistance for higher education, marked major moves toward providing the material assistance the Truman Report implicitly promised (Brock, 2010). To qualify for the funding, states were required to design coordinating commissions that would provide systematic and standardized guidelines for the development of higher education. What resulted were the beginnings of more comprehensive master plans that helped to guide community college expansion at the state level (Cohen, 2001).

For community colleges, the period of the 1960s was a period of planning, development, and standardization. Efforts often focused on costs as states determined the best ways to help interested students access community college education. States made and executed plans to pay some manner of operating costs, to approve the use of property taxes for education, and to provide matching funds for full-time student enrollment. In all cases, state plans reflected a nearly universal goal that aimed for 95 percent of the population to be within commuting distance to a community college (Cohen, 2011). Although access continued to be the order of the day, state plans to facilitate access could not alone force unity. Widely held views amongst local communities asserted that community colleges should be driven by "local needs and conditions" rather than by state or federal control (Cohen, 2001,

p. 13). Accordingly, pressing questions began to be asked about who should control the growth of community colleges and how.

❧

Community colleges in the postwar years continued to be positioned as transitional and flexible in their institutional offerings. In addition to supplying students with a greater continuity between secondary and tertiary schooling and offering closer proximity to communities than could be had at traditional, 4-year institutions, community colleges offered the wide access deemed American education's most emphatic goal. Access was the guiding force, so much so that sociologists Richard Arum and Josipa Roksa (2011) claimed access as the distillation of the entire century's educative concern: "public and policy discussions of higher education over the course of the twentieth century have focused on one issue in particular: access" (p. 34).

Despite Arum and Roksa's argument, however, in the latter half of the twentieth century the focused attention on the promise of access began to give way, incrementally at first but then more and more, to a more focused attention on achievement (Bailey, Jaggars, & Jenkins, 2015). As community colleges attracted the many new students seeking higher education, the colleges were criticized for their "incomplete functionality and contradictory effects" (Dougherty, 1994, p. 35). This was particularly the case when it came to the students—often nontraditional students and already underserved minorities—who sought access but who were unable to secure the achievement that access to higher education implicitly promised. Providing access for all prospective students was greatly emphasized (and all but legislated in the Truman Report), but as the twentieth century progressed, the material consequences of ensuring access prompted scrutiny of community colleges, community college students, and standards at the state and federal level.

Chapter 2

The 1950s and Beyond

Anyone Can Enter,
But Can Everyone Achieve?

The major uptick in student enrollment subsequent to the G.I. Bill and the federally mandated emphasis on access were prime contributors to America's explosive higher education scene during the midcentury. However, the social foment of the 1960s that insisted on the critical import of democracy and equality was another major influence. The presence of women, African Americans, and other ethnic minorities at the institutions from which they had been barred informed the missions of all American higher education institutions (Kim & Rury, 2007). It especially impacted the missions and subsequent efforts of community colleges. Thanks in large part to the huge numbers of students, particularly untraditional students, community colleges experienced an unprecedented leap in popularity that fueled their growth, their legitimacy, and their challenges.

∾

Despite the precious little ink spilled in the Truman Commission's 1947 report on women's presence in higher education or on the active dissent over African Americans' *access* to higher education, virtually all American schools opened their doors to more woman and nonwhite students after the Civil Rights Act of 1964. Consequently, after the act's passage, untraditional students matriculated at all tertiary institutions. Given the foundational open-access policies at community colleges and the Truman Commission's insistence that community colleges remain open to all, the community colleges were often the first educational home for incoming populations.

The popularity of the colleges reflected the particular niche the schools continued working to fill. The college's popularity among women offers an illustrative example. Women began to arrive *en masse* at all higher education institutions during and after the 1970s (Deegan & Tillery, 1985). Within a few short years, women constituted the majority of all enrollees in tertiary schools (Snyder & Dillow, 2011). Often, women were particularly attracted to community colleges because community colleges offered unparalleled flexibility.

The flexibility was a pointed manifestation of the colleges' attempts to be all things to all potential students. Here again we see that the contradictions that characterized community colleges' founding and evolution functioned as a major reason for their appeal (Bers, 1983). The disparate schools that made up the community college sector and the wide focus at these different schools on occupational *and* continuing education *and* transfer-oriented programs encouraged, and in fact necessitated, student-led and student-motivated curricular choices. The necessity neither appealed to nor benefited everybody, but it certainly appealed to women, particularly women over 35 or women for whom the cost, location, or requirements at more traditional institutions were out of reach. Consequently, beginning in the 1960s, community colleges provided the most convenient avenue by which women could meet their widely variable educational needs without infringing on their social and familial obligations (Deegan & Tillery, 1985).

African Americans of the same time period also found a home in community colleges, but they faced a very different situation. Unlike the women who purposefully sought out the special offerings available at community colleges, African Americans frequently arrived at community colleges out of necessity. It was not the institutional flexibility or part-time options that were especially attractive; up to the passage of the Civil Rights Act (and by many accounts long after it) Jim Crow officially ruled institutions in the South (and sometimes appeared to unofficially rule many higher education institutions in the North). Seats at traditional institutions—for incoming African American veterans looking to access higher education after the passage of the G.I. Bill, for example—were severely limited (The Journal of Blacks in Higher Education, 2003).

Further obstructing African Americans' participation in higher education was the general inaccessibility of Historically Black Colleges and Universities. The HBCUs could not provide much of an alternative for many African Americans because the institutions were initially located almost uniformly in the South and were thus too far removed geographically to constitute an economically feasible choice (The Journal of Blacks in Higher Education, 2003). In addition, HBCUs were selective and were in no position to accommodate the overwhelming number of interested students. Because of this, many African Americans found in community colleges the only institution that could or even would enable their access to higher education. From 1960 to 1970, community colleges became the population's requisite institutional home, particularly as African American high school graduation rates increased (Karen, 1991).

❧

The access that community colleges continued to privilege, and the relatively low tuitions they touted meant that community college rosters swelled with women, African Americans, Hispanics, other underserved minorities, and other untraditional students. As a consequence, enrollment skyrocketed from five hundred thousand in 1960 to over 2 million in 1970 (Cohen, Brawer, & Kisker, 2013). In an echo of education's expansion in the early twentieth century, the huge numbers promoted community college growth and an institutional claim to correspondent legitimacy. In fact, Thelin reported (2011) that this rapid, incredibly dramatic expansion led to a kind of validity that vaunted the college to a position of a "distinctively American institution" (p. 260).

As in the earlier postwar decades, the uniquely American sector of community colleges appeared to be on track for fulfilling Dewey's vision of democratic education. The sector was growing fast and was able to boast campuses that were "among the best in the land" (Deegan & Tillery, 1985, p. 16), that served a major portion of the population seeking higher education—nearly 30 percent (Kim & Rury, 2007)—and that offered top-notch educational services to students often unable to otherwise access tertiary education. For community colleges, the 1960s and 1970s were generally a time of "great confidence" (Deegan & Tillery, 1985, p. 16). The Carnegie Commission on Higher Education repeated these boasts in its special report, *The Open-Door Colleges*. On the report's first page, its authors declared that community colleges had finally "proved their worth."

But almost as soon as they were articulated, the heady expectations for community colleges began to weaken. The reasons were varied. First, community colleges still operated on the proverbial *outside*. The overwhelming popularity of the colleges led to the institution's tacit acceptance among America's other higher education institutions. However, the popularity meant that the colleges were increasingly placed under a microscope that magnified what would become stubbornly persistent institutional challenges. Foremost among these challenges were the continued lack of strong organizational identity and the perceptions of lackluster student—and thus institutional—achievement.

Second, and contributing to the persistent outsider status, the community college's reason-for-being—its promise of open access—created a raft of related institutional difficulties. Primarily, the open-access policies that made community colleges such an appropriate home for untraditional students ensured an incredibly diverse student body. The diversity was a welcome manifestation of the community college's democratic ethos. Yet as the student body grew, community colleges found it more and more difficult to meet the different students' variable needs.

This chapter will demonstrate the obvious trend that, despite growing pains, community colleges became increasingly popular as the postwar years passed and the twentieth century progressed. Continued growth looked a lot like past growth: the challenges associated with the institution's outsider status and its open-access policies did not resolve. Instead, the growth worked to deepen an apparent intransigence. Community colleges were still characterized by an uncertain organizational identity that reverberated in the uncertain academic achievements of its students.

The challenges became obvious in the midcentury and beyond, but they were not initially directly addressed by leaders, administrators, and policymakers. In fact, most of the people associated with community colleges took the opposite track. Investigators like the authors of *The Open-Door Colleges*, for example, simply doubled down on access as a unifying, problem-solving principle. The report's authors argued that if the community college sector wanted to continue to track the upward trajectory facilitated by the institution's increased popularity (especially among untraditional and underserved minority students) the sector would have to continue strenuous efforts to fulfill the open-access mission.

Consequently, rather than discuss meeting the on-the-ground needs of the exploding community college student population, the report drove home an argument for the continuation of service expansion, even recommending a name change to reflect the argument. The extension for which community colleges must strive, wrote the authors, meant that the colleges should operate not as simple *community* colleges but as *comprehensive* community colleges. *Comprehensive community colleges* offered a totalizing handle by which to describe total and totalizing institutions; these institutions connected to one another via the broad mission through which they offered an ever wider variety of educational services, including transfer, general, remedial, occupational, cultural and continuing education, to the largest possible variety of young people and adults.

Of course, an explicitly designated comprehensive curriculum was probably always the likely path of the community college, which was designed from its inception (if not always purposefully), to be as accessible, as flexible, and as encompassing as institutionally possible. But such a far-ranging, comprehensive focus did not provide the organizational identity that community colleges need in the middle of the twentieth century. It instead worked to aggravate the institutional challenges to defining and facilitating identity and to defining and assessing broad standards for achievement. In this way, the Carnegie Commission's reinforcement of *comprehensiveness* amounted to a federally authorized extension of the community colleges' past into its future. Only as comprehensive, the report implied, would the community college be positioned to fulfill (or at least better able to more accurately articulate) its attempts to be all things to all potential students.

In some ways, we might view the continued federally authorized emphasis on access as setting up the community college sector for its contemporary failures. First, the attention to access diffused rather than tightened organizational focus, and obscured rather than clarified the directions in which community colleges could and should develop. The enforced comprehensiveness actually underlined—rather than helped to solve—a continued lack of uniformity, and failed completely to provide an overarching or foundational structure through which community colleges could be more efficiently affiliated. *Comprehensive* was generally a useful signifier, and the commission's backing suggested an authoritative and persuasive means by which the institutions called "community colleges" could be brought together. However, without more informed directions on how to enact these efforts, the unity was ultimately only arbitrary.

Second, and perhaps more insidious (particularly given the fallout of the accountability movement, discussed below), the continued strenuous federal support of expansiveness reinforced a problematic opposition to exclusivity, which was unfortunately aligned with achievement. To put it another way, for all the attention given the issue of access, a discussion about achievement was mostly absent. The result? A continuation of the community college's uneven trajectory driven by a sustained, national-level dialogue that emphasized the extensiveness of access over the exclusivity of achievement.

While the dialogue may not have posed as much of a problem when community colleges were still working to better occupy an institutional niche among American educational institutions, this changed pretty dramatically as community colleges grew and multiplied in the 1960s and 1970s. Once the colleges became the educational home to so many more students, and once the colleges commanded so many more resources for institutional operation, the need to pair wide access with a standardized definition of and pathway toward reachable achievement became more obviously necessary.

Leaders and administrators, for their part, responded to the growth of community colleges and its accompanying pressures in specific ways. In general, leaders, administrators, and policymakers recognized, even if only implicitly, the need to accommodate the continued exhortation to access and the as-yet-unspoken but obvious need to provide navigable paths to achievement. They saw that the many new and untraditional students at their schools required physical, academic, social, and financial accommodation and that these kinds of accommodations had to happen along many fronts. Gaps in student preparation and institutional funding, for example, had to be identified and bridged, resources had to be made available, facilities had to be built, and effective curricula and student services had to be developed and dispersed. Above all, the means for defining and analyzing success had to be determined. These gaps existed at many community colleges and indicated that to address what was essentially a systemic need, community colleges must integrate as part of a system.

∾

For good and for ill, the system was to be the overly diffuse system of American postsecondary education. Before the 1960s, tertiary education in America was a disorganized affair. The work among community colleges to develop a better, more efficient, more communicative, and more connected organizational and administrative structure had already begun—albeit rather cautiously and as a consequence of federal mandates—during the 1960s. The Higher Education Act (HEA) of 1965 mobilized states to create master plans and establish standardized, uniform governance, but it was only the first in a series of similar prompts. Later amendments to the HEA more emphatically drove the planning and the organizational and administrative standardization that justified a claim to a national higher education *system*. Indeed, before the passage of federal amendments, institutional efforts to accommodate the new growth in student populations revealed that the so-called system possessed so many inconsistencies that it thwarted the very concept of systematization.

The HEA amendments clarified at the federal level a national trend: in general, there were more students, and this meant there were more students' needs. More students' needs more clearly revealed what had always been the case—that the system of national education was still very much a work in progress. The HEA amendments therefore provided the guidance necessary to clean up higher education's general messiness by suggesting methods for crossing the deep divides separating different schools (and occasionally backing up suggestions with the promise of federal funding) (Tollefson, 1994). While the federal efforts were generally new, they continued down the familiar path previously hewn by the Morrill Acts and the G.I. Bill. Symbolically, they offered a federal-level indication of the import of higher education. Practically, they stood as an effort to arrange and facilitate increased access to this important, although not national, resource. Operationally, they enforced the value of *all* tertiary educational options. Ultimately, they attested to the depth of the need to consolidate higher education into a more meaningful and far more efficient system.

Community colleges benefited from the amendments' attempts to shape a system, and from the language promoted therein that reinforced the colleges' claim to equal participation. Specifically, the amendments discarded the disjointed conversations fostered by a too-loose "higher education" descriptor, and adopted the more encompassing language associated with "postsecondary." The simple shift in language, like the shifts in language that preceded it (from *junior* to *community* college, for example), facilitated a helpful blurring of the distinctions between the kind of higher education offered at traditional 4-year institutions and the kinds of education offered at institutions like community colleges.

Our contemporary terminology makes it clear that the amendments expedited the general adoption of *postsecondary schooling* as the preferred verbiage for the varied and various tertiary institutions. Community colleges, despite their growth, still operated in a liminal space, but the HEA's amendments and their language advanced the institutions' conscription in what was still a constellation, or a proto-system, of postsecondary schools. By facilitating "nationwide acceptance and improved understanding," the amendments laid the foundation for coherent coordination and tipped a hat to the radically different but still valid and vital forms that postsecondary schooling could take (Martorana, 1974, p. 4).

∼

As was the case with the Carnegie Commission's rhetoric, however, language alone could not quiet the implicit questions of inferiority and even legitimacy that beset community colleges in the wake of their popularity. The colleges may have boasted higher enrollment rates, received more federal attention, and displayed stronger connections to postsecondary institutions, but a continued emphasis on a mission to be all things to all potential students meant that the institution continued its efforts to fulfill an incredibly difficult, perhaps even impossible, task. Despite its huge growth and its participation in America's postsecondary system, the institutions continued to struggle for an organizational identity that took its specific challenges into account. Consequently, the institutions also continued to negotiate a general perception as both outside and as less-than.

Ironically, this stubborn sense that community colleges provided a lesser education was crystallized by the very amendments that brought community colleges into the postsecondary fold. The HEA amendments were contentious for many reasons, but leaders and administrators specifically balked at the apparent federal emphasis on large-scale, inter-institutional *planning* and *coordination* (Martorana, 1974). Those aforementioned commissions—called the 1202s because they were established by section 1202 of the HEA—were the sole state-specific committees charged with overseeing federal-level but state-specific comprehensive postsecondary development. Naturally, the committees were suspect (Martorana, 1974, p. 9).

While the widespread federal attention on postsecondary schooling was generally welcome, particularly because leaders and administrators hoped that the attention might lead to substantive federal funding, the 1202s ignited suspicions about assimilation. Many leaders and administrators did not want community colleges and traditional institutions to occupy the same postsecondary plane. Consequently, efforts that looked like an attempt to equalize the postsecondary environment through broad administration or sweeping resource allocation were resisted.

Probably unsurprisingly, it was not only administrators at traditional 4-year colleges who flinched. Community college administrators felt the same way, and often for the same reasons: the planning and management efforts of postsecondary institutions were powerfully informed by *local* not by universal need. Four-year university administrators who did not want federal oversight expressed opposition to an expansive focus that might limit their concerns. At the same time, community college administrators who did not want the needs of their institutions overshadowed and usurped by the larger, more traditional institutions in their state also winced (Martorana, 1974).

Like so much else regarding community college identity, the issue was complicated: federal interest was necessary to help institutions better correlate their postsecondary efforts, to better face the challenges associated with changing student populations, and to better prepare for a future in which sustained student growth was not a certainty. But few postsecondary leaders or administrators perceived tangible benefits to smoothing over the vast differences between the many and disparate institutions that populated the postsecondary landscape. Broad systematization made obvious sense, but any effort perceived as *leveling* postsecondary access and making the varieties of postsecondary education commensurate was more alarming. While few administrators could afford to deny the possibility of participating in and maximizing the return on federal and especially state resources, just as many simultaneously felt the import of institutional autonomy and feared the gradual loss of local control (Cohen, 2010).

Crucially, the need for coordination (which became more pressing as the twentieth century wore on) ultimately overcame this resistance. Despite reservations, federal plans were ultimately largely successful. Even when planning efforts were divorced from federal funding, states increasingly complied with the federal encouragement to develop large-scale, statewide postsecondary development efforts. There really was no other choice: too many schools and too many students required more efficient and less redundant resource allocation. As a consequence, state concerns increasingly subsumed local agendas. Although institutional administrators expressed unease with what they perhaps perceived to be federal meddling, far more comprehensive state planning for all postsecondary institutions became the norm, not the exception (Cohen, 2010; Martorana, 1974, p. 14; Tollefson, 1994).

∾

Although they worked mostly successfully to bring community colleges into the postsecondary system, the HEA amendments, particularly the planning and development efforts inaugurated by the 1202s, also reinforced the differences that continued to separate community colleges from their traditional counterparts. On the one hand, the federal attention spoke to the community colleges' institutional popularity and lent credence to a longstanding claim to postsecondary validity. On the other hand, that attention provoked the expression of a discomfort that reflected some of the real-world difficulties in yoking community colleges' needs—and students—to the needs and students of more traditional institutions. Although for community colleges, the contradiction was merely one of many, it illustrated that for community colleges *contradiction* was and would continue to be a permanent condition.

In fact, *contradiction* undeniably fueled the two conflicting stories about community colleges that emerged in the later years of the twentieth century. The first story narrated an increase in enrollment, attention, and funding that allowed the community college sector to come into its own. The colleges were able to better realize their open-access mission and related policies through a more diverse student population, more comprehensive curricular offerings, and relatively more connected administrations. The new developments, aided in part by federal and especially state planning efforts, ensured that the sector claimed a progressively meaningful and stronger position in a nascent but powerful American postsecondary system (Deegan & Tillery, 1985).

The second story was not nearly as optimistic. In this narrative, community colleges experienced a continuation and deepening of the tensions that accompanied their foundation and early development. The huge numbers of new and untraditional students fostered the continuation of uneven growth, and the increased federal attention revealed a widespread dissatisfaction with the community college's claim to equal footing with more traditional 4-year schools. With the intensifying pressure of increasing popularity and attention, the institution revealed a fundamental inability to make good on its mission: it was fundamentally *unable* to be all things to all potential students. As a consequence, it was in danger of reneging on the democratic promise out of which the institution had been born.

∿

Further confounding these larger institutional contradictions were the more local, internal contradictions that characterized community college programs. At many community colleges, the comprehensive curricular focus was generally divided among the occupational-oriented programs, which gained in popularity during the postwar years, and the transfer-oriented programs, which aligned the colleges with more traditional postsecondary schools. Although this same divide seemed to have been ably negotiated in the first half of the century, it became decisive and tension-filled in the century's second half (Brint & Karabel, 1989). During this time period, the majority of community colleges continued to shift their focus on terminal and vocational training. Transfer rates consequently dipped to historic lows. After this shift, the *divide* became more of a resounding *breach*.

Of particular concern was the increased interest on the part of community colleges in answering community needs (and shoring up institutional funding) through contract training programs. The programs were established in partnership or at the behest of local businesses that sought trained employees for particular work. Accordingly, the programs seemed especially keyed to addressing community college challenges (Brint & Karabel, 1989; Gabert, 1990). Because the programs reinforced the colleges' occupational focus, attracted untraditional students, and met local communities' needs, the development was, for many community college leaders and administrators, quite welcome. The Carnegie Commission, Edmund Gleazer, and the AACC, for example, recognized the programs as a successful part of the wide effort to ensure that community colleges met student demand and that the institutions would be sustainable in the far more competitive years to come.

But the strong new alliances also strengthened old criticisms, especially those that saw the programs as keeping community colleges firmly outside the postsecondary fold and those that saw the programs as reiterating the cooling-out function by which community colleges were again accused of curtailing student options and reproducing the American social structure of limited social mobility. College leaders and administrators developed contract-training programs at least in part to stake out navigable paths to achievement, but the solution was deemed by many to be insufficient. Further, the deeper dependence on vocationalism at the expense of less remunerative but still valuable transfer-oriented courses was criticized as unreasonable. Ultimately, the focus on terminal training (despite its ties to community businesses and therefore community jobs) was not viewed as beneficial to all (Pincus, 1986).

In fact, despite the institutional commitment to terminal and vocational work, transfer rates continued to symbolize the "academic purposes" of many community colleges (Grubb, 1991, p. 195). As such, the rates seemed to suggest community colleges' ability to promote a more egalitarian education. After all, if the colleges were unable to pave the way to a 4-year degree for students who sought it, the colleges were hardly offering the broad access their missions advertised. And the number of students seeking a baccalaureate degree was not insignificant; many students who arrived at community colleges in the latter half of the twentieth century indicated that they wanted to receive a baccalaureate degree (Grubb, 1991).

Critics therefore viewed the vocational offerings that eclipsed transfer-oriented options as responsible for maintaining community colleges' less-than status and for contributing to the social stratification that barred the equal rights seemingly promised by earlier civil rights movements (Beach, 2011; Brint & Karabel, 1989; Karabel, 1986; Pincus, 1986; Zwerling, 1986). In this, too, community colleges were caught in a contradiction, and again they were considered to possibly be failing their democratic function. According to this line of argument, by limiting possible pathways to achievement to occupational programs, the students who most needed the access to the education provided by community colleges (and those students very often included overrepresented underserved minorities) were only able to avail themselves of a limited number of professions. Unsurprisingly, these professions did not promise a certain or high return (Dougherty, 1994; Grubb, 1991; Pascarella & Terenzini, 1991).

The necessity to be all things to all potential students ensured that the struggle for curricular balance at community colleges would remain unresolved. In fact, despite the past outcry and the ongoing criticism, a vocational focus became a major focus at community colleges, and many onlookers viewed the substantive move to be a reflection of both institutional and student interest. The shift was also viewed as part of a broader trend that indicated a societal pause in the previously unrestrained belief, especially amongst the American middle class, that a postsecondary baccalaureate degree provided a one-way ticket to a better life.

Although this belief was entirely lacking during the latter half of the nineteenth century, by the latter half of the twentieth century it was so entrenched that postsecondary institutions of all stripes struggled to maintain a reputation when the market that had once handsomely rewarded graduates faltered. When the American job market stalled in the 1970s and then again in the 1980s and fewer graduates were rewarded for their undergraduate efforts, it became easier to consider that postsecondary degrees were perhaps less valuable than they once had been (Bailey, Kienzl, & Marcotte, 2004; Pincus, 1980).

The skepticism was partly fueled by the ambiguity around the many, sometimes unspoken, questions, about the devalued economic benefit of a degree (Brint & Karabel, 1989). It was also fueled by an increased focus, at both the national and local level, on the rising costs of attending a postsecondary school and securing a degree. In addition to community colleges, all post-secondary institutions had experienced spikes in enrollment in the previous decades, but the growth in college costs during the 1980s far outpaced the growth in the median family income, (Lazerson, 1998). A college degree was still absolutely necessary to secure something better than low-wage employment (and in fact, it was more necessary than ever), but the degree's cost no longer appeared to be as closely matched to a correspondent wage or salary (Brint & Karabel, 1989; Lazerson, 1998).

∼

The depressed job market and the relatively new questions about the worth of a postsecondary education should have been an unmitigated boon to community colleges. As baccalaureate degrees were perceived as less valuable, the stranglehold that traditional 4-year institutions had on postsecondary legitimacy loosened, and the traditional institutions began to appear as offering a far less commonsense approach to earning a postsecondary education. Community colleges once again were positioned to capitalize on the breadth of their programs and curricular offerings, and the increased emphasis on a particular vocational focus.

Of course, the boon was not at all straightforward. While increased skepticism of the value of traditional postsecondary institutions favored community colleges, the skepticism did not redound in a material increase at community colleges. Instead, it redounded in the beginnings of an "accountability movement" (Green, 1981, p. 68). In fact, the skepticism surrounding postsecondary schools culminated in questions in the face of insufficient information on postsecondary standards and student and institutional achievement. The lack of general data had already provoked a widespread call for information about *all* institutional and student achievement. The accountability movement would characterize the American postsecondary system from the second half of the twentieth century all the way up to today.

Community colleges, which had become more attractive to students and families disillusioned by the high cost of attending a more traditional institution, were not exempt—were in fact incredibly *nonexempt*—from the movement in which all postsecondary institutions were, or would soon be, embroiled. Subsequent to the relatively new focus on achievement, community colleges especially found themselves on the hook to prove measures of attainment that were more universal and objective than what had once been signified by a good job.

The accountability movement impacted community colleges in complicated ways (and not least because the movement still informs our everyday institutional concerns). First, community colleges faced reporting challenges that their more traditional counterparts did not. As we already well know, the colleges' overwhelming emphasis on access and comprehensiveness gave rise to unprecedented, unchecked institutional and curricular diversity. This ensured that most data points that might have been able to answer to achievement and prove accountability were nonstandard, that most knowledge was difficult to systematically gather, and that most information was institution-specific and was retrieved regionally, not nationally (Grubb, 1991). The lack of uniformity, which could be and often was translated as an inherent lack of standards, also translated to a dearth of actual, comparable knowledge regarding achievement (Mellow & Heelan, 2008).

Second, without universally marked out definitions for standards and student attainment, community colleges were increasingly held accountable by students, taxpayers, and policymakers to prove their worth. It had become pretty clear that the institutional ascent experienced by community colleges in the 1960s and 1970s did not always or even usually redound in students' easily determinable success or measurable achievement in the 1980s, 1990s, and beyond (Mellow & Heelan, 2008). The declining transfer rates at community colleges supported the observations (Grubb, 1991). Although this particular data point was problematic because so many community colleges had long emphasized vocational and continuing education services over a more transfer-oriented education, transfer rates still represented a meaningful measure in the minds of many leaders, administrators, policymakers, and students.

Third, the institutional variability that made data collection and comparison so challenging contributed to the flexibility that appealed to the colleges' often untraditional and often part-time students. Put another way, the variability among community colleges was reinforced, as it always had been, by the colleges' popularity. The increasing numbers of women who in the 1960s and 1970s sought a postsecondary education that would fit their lifestyles had already illustrated this, as did the increasing numbers of untraditional students in the 1980s and 1990s. These students were frequently drawn from local populations, and they frequently looked to postsecondary education to address extremely localized, extremely disparate concerns. They often chose educational paths that differed, usually markedly, from the paths taken by students at more traditional postsecondary schools. In so doing, they thwarted easy answers to questions of achievement and the compilation of data.

The giant influx of students previously unaccepted at more traditional institutions were therefore never able to materially shift the view of community colleges as less-than. In fact, from the birth of the community college as an institution, the influx of *these very* students proved an obstacle to accountability and achievement measures. Their ever larger numbers at the end of the twentieth century ultimately (if only inadvertently) supported a reprisal of the argument that community colleges were capably fulfilling a protective function for more prestigious postsecondary schools (Dougherty, Bork, & Natow, 2009).

In the last years of the twentieth century, community colleges continued working to consolidate their organizational identity and to define, gather, and analyze data on achievement. The colleges did this not by ceasing but by *increasing* their responsiveness to their disparate students. Regardless of the difficulty in measuring and generalizing these students' various levels of achievement, and regardless of how problematic this difficulty was to community colleges' institutional reputation, the colleges continued catering to student and community needs. Doing so obviously fulfilled the community colleges' open-access mission, but it also importantly ensured, at least in part, the institution's democratic, egalitarian foundation to educate *all* students.

～

Doing so also supported community colleges' bottom line. The more students who gained entry to community colleges, the more community colleges' rosters benefited. Such students, particularly students who stayed to achieve their goals, provided an excellent foundation for community colleges' long-term economic feasibility. The stability was important and proved even more so as the traditional student cohort of 18- to 24-year-olds declined or plateaued and as state fiscal contributions became scarce (Lazerson, 1998).

Financial sustenance was often a product of student populations, but it was not necessarily a direct product. Over the course of the twentieth century, community colleges, like many postsecondary institutions, became more reliant on more generous federal funding and state appropriations. Although federal funding for postsecondary education had initially been slow to appear (except through federal research grant programs), it became much more meaningful after the 1970s (Thelin, 2011).

Among other efforts, the federal government implemented the Basic Education Opportunities Grants (better known as the Pell Grants) program. The awards supplied portable entitlement aid to qualifying students. Recipients were able to use their grants at any accredited postsecondary institution, including community colleges. In addition to Pell Grants, other federal programs that benefited community colleges appeared, including the Supplemental Educational Opportunity Grants, the College Work Study Program, and National Direct Student Loans. The programs awarded transferable vouchers, grants, jobs, and loans to students, and allowed them to attend whatever school students deemed able to provide them with the best fit (Gilbert & Heller, 2013).

Community colleges were immensely helped by the federal awards, subsidies, and loans, and not just materially. The money that supported students in their pursuit of community college education reinforced the institutions' still-controversial participation in the American postsecondary system and suggested the institution's claim to somewhat equal standing with more traditional schools. This was the case even when community colleges received money designated for vocational development, such as through the Vocational Act of 1963 and its subsequent amendments. The money, obviously allotted for vocational education and almost uniformly directed to community colleges, helped to shape community college program offerings and aided the colleges' continued development. Like federal *attention* (but far better in material terms), federal *funding* was a relative windfall in the search for stability among postsecondary schools. Students were better able to matriculate to the institutions of their choice and were therefore able to contribute to institutional and student growth and success.

Naturally, the more money the government spent on education, the more closely educational institutions were held to public and legislative account and the more deeply entrenched the accountability movement became. As the accountability movement began to function as a permanent context for postsecondary institutions, it ushered in the possibility that funding, historically dependent on enrollment numbers, might become more intimately tied to student and institutional performance.

Given the continued difficulty in defining, securing, and assessing achievement, the stakes of this connection were (and still are) particularly high for community colleges. The stakes were also particularly high because the colleges were far more dependent than traditional 4-year institutions on both the portable student support extended by the federal government and on state taxes, usually property taxes, and state appropriations.

As has been the case throughout its institutional development, the community college often faced pressure to prove to taxpayers and policymakers *particular* worth. This was a consequence of the wide access that implicitly promised to be all things to all students; it was a consequence of a heavy draw on federal and state resources; and it was a consequence of the institution's comprehensive focus, which rather insidiously suggests to policymakers that community colleges might inefficiently reproduce coursework that could be better completed elsewhere. Where curricular offerings appeared to overlap with other institutions (remedial courses reproducing high school curriculums, or transfer-oriented courses reproducing 4-year schools' foundational courses, for example), the offerings at community colleges could be considered redundant, superfluous, or simply a waste of resources.

Many of these fiscal challenges were faced by all postsecondary institutions: in fact all postsecondary institutions worked to navigate waters made turbulent by accountability and financial matters (Thelin, 2011). Martorana (1974), for example, argued that postsecondary institutions were on the defensive as early as the 1970s and struggled thereafter to accommodate intensifying pressure to display a record of achievement and requisite evidence that the institutions had not expanded too aggressively and were sustainable and valuable. The pressure amounted to an overwhelming emphasis on reported statistics, an emphasis that gained steam as taxpayers, policymakers, communities, and students posed progressively difficult questions to all postsecondary institutions (McCarton, 1983).

For community colleges, the challenges were certainly not new. As this discussion in this and the previous chapter have shown, community colleges were born out of contradictions that have reappeared at each stage of the college's institutional development. That the contradiction has proven so difficult to resolve is hardly surprising. As the twentieth century drew to a close, the questions asked by taxpayers, policymakers, communities, and students reflected the questions that had accompanied community colleges from the beginning: namely, did the colleges capably fulfill the role legislated on their behalf, did the colleges provide access to an effective and comprehensive (but also specialized) curriculum to a huge variety of learners, and did the colleges graduate people prepared to enter the field or role of their choice? Could community colleges deliver on their democratic promise and be all things to all potential students?

Perhaps in an implicit and disappointed response to these and other questions posed in the late years of the twentieth century, government funding for community colleges—and for all higher education—declined (Lazerson, 1998).

~

The end of the twentieth century most certainly *did not* mark an end to the challenges that beset community colleges. Rather, the opposite was true. By 2000, the colleges were still cycling through by-now familiar difficulties associated with bridging the divide separating the planning and execution of a still broadly comprehensive focus, the divide separating an unprecedentedly large and unmanageable number of vocational-oriented and transfer-oriented programs, and the divide separating the persistent emphasis on broad access *and* on reachable achievement. While there is absolutely no doubt that community colleges occupied a crucial component of the contemporary American postsecondary education system, the colleges continued to struggle to define their institutions, their mission, their students, and their measures of achievement.

This struggle continues, sometimes inexplicably, to promote growth. Despite the issues posed by temporary enrollment setbacks, increased competition for untraditional students from both traditional 4-year schools and proprietary schools, and an ever-increasing scrutiny that will probably never diminish, the growth of community colleges has continued almost unabated. Community colleges continue to be absolutely critical to the American postsecondary system, and as more students seek out postsecondary schooling, the colleges' importance will continue to increase. But continued growth remains only a small part of the solution to repairing community colleges and reinstating the democratic promise on which the colleges are founded.

As we look to the future, we must recognize that we may never solve our most intransigent challenges. We may never conclusively resolve the tension between access and achievement, for example, without seriously undermining the foundational missions of our schools. At the same time, we cannot stand idly by as a historical emphasis on access is met with only a shallow (if enthusiastic) assessment of achievement. We cannot stand idly by and allow community colleges to price out the most vulnerable populations or allow our colleges to fail to contribute to the meaningful education of these populations.

It is past time to revisit and revise the promise community colleges extend our students and our communities. We must go beyond recognizing the heterogeneity of the needs that characterize our diverse students and turn instead to the models that offer a way forward. While an emphasis on remediating academic deficiencies has long preoccupied community college leaders, administrators, and policymakers, we must now also turn our attention to the social and financial needs of our students. This, I believe, is the key to institutional and student success.

The previous chapters have established an accounting of the community college's crucial place in American education and have identified the historical roots of the stubborn problems that continue to hold back our schools. In the next two chapters, I turn to a discussion of the experiential and competency-based models for pedagogy and student support services that will equip community college students for educational and professional success.

Chapter 3

Repairing the Broken Promise

Creating a Culture of Care
in the Community College Setting

In my first two chapters, I described the complicated historical development of community colleges and showed that community colleges, from their inception, have been marked by somewhat repetitive contradictions. The institution was born to bridge the yawning gap between secondary and tertiary schools; it worked to buttress that bridge amidst the turbulence of the Great Depression, WWII, and the explosive social unrest of the 60s and 70s; and it expanded during the dynamic and ongoing accountability and multicultural movements of the 1990s and 2000s. Recent years have provided a similarly dramatic context, but today, community colleges must work to negotiate the radically shifting technological and social landscapes of the twenty-first century.

To navigate this environment, contemporary community college leaders, administrators, teachers, and policymakers must continue strenuous efforts to negotiate the cross currents of the institution's still ultimately contradictory position (Dougherty, 1991). In fact, its position is more contradictory than ever before. Access, which was a major component of the democratic promise that accompanied the institution's founding, has, over the years, morphed from a guiding inspiration to a required mandate. Community colleges were and still are motivated, encouraged, and implicitly or explicitly required at both a local and national level to operate with a wide-open door.

Contemporary community colleges therefore continue to offer the most generous point of entry to incoming students seeking a postsecondary education. However, today's community colleges do not consistently or systematically deliver the high-quality education sought by students pursuing a postsecondary education. The failure should not be surprising: it is a structural consequence of the exhortation to access. By implicitly and usually explicitly promising to provide a home to *all* potential students, community colleges promise to meet their ever more widely variable academic, financial, and social needs. Community colleges promise to enable all students to meet their divergent goals for education; consequently, community colleges promise to help all students achieve their dreams.

Our contemporary colleges simply cannot meet the enormousness of this promise (in part because of the relatively little support our schools are given, a point to which I will return in Chapter 5). While we have been able to hold open our doors to all interested students, we have not been able to provide navigable pathways to achievement across the stunning variety of programs and courses our contemporary colleges now offer (Bailey, Jaggars, & Jenkins, 2015). The failure has obviously impacted the institution in negative ways, most glaringly in low retention and completion rates. In fact, statistics compiled by the National Student Clearinghouse indicate that only about 40 percent of incoming students reach completion in six years. By the arguably less accurate statistics compiled by the U.S. Department of Education, that number is closer to 20 percent (Juskiewicz, 2014).

When community colleges fail, the institutions suffer, but the *students* absorb the majority of the impact. Imagine the difficulty faced by someone who considers community college the key—perhaps the only key—to a better life. She is willing to put in the work (which, as we recall, very often includes remedial work that does not clearly contribute to award or program completion) and to make the social and financial sacrifices (which, as we know, can be considerable and sometimes insurmountable). But after too many months or years spent finding her footing on an achievable path to completion that will put her on track for a higher paying job, she realizes that she just cannot continue making the same sacrifices. For this student, and for the many who are also in her position, completion is out of reach.

Every single one of the 13 million students who attend a community college comes to college with individual struggles, hopes, and dreams. But too many are thwarted on the path to achievement. While their failure is of course a personal failure, it is an institutional failure, too. It impacts families and schools, but it also impacts our nation and our economy. In fact, community college students make up a major part of the American workforce; their growing numbers augur the future of the American—which is to say the global—marketplace. If our colleges cannot enable our students to succeed, then our students cannot become productive members of the national economy, and the national economy cannot thrive.

My voice is certainly not the only contributor to this argument. President Obama argued in his presentation of the American Graduation Initiative (2009) that community college students make up America's future global workforce. Their somewhat newfound importance is a consequence of shifting winds of employment: jobs that require an associate's degree are rising and are expected to continue to rise quickly. According to the federal government's view, the trend makes community colleges a key institution for the future of the American economy. This perspective matches my own: the success of community college students is not just an institutional imperative, it is a national one.

Although the struggle to deliver on the community college promise of wide access and attainable achievement has received recent attention from researchers and policymakers, effective solutions that can meaningfully impact a critical number of students (and thus a critical number of institution) have not yet appeared. Community colleges still try and often fail to develop and implement the intensive and intrusive advisement needed to guide community college students through the difficult paths to completion. Community colleges still attempt (and not always successfully) to provide meaningful support services to students who are willing to work but who face sometimes insurmountable obstacles. Community colleges still work, although to a limited extent (given often absent funding), to enact and benefit from pedagogical research to improve the teaching of underprepared students.

I believe that today we must work to ensure that the present attention of leaders, administrators, faculty members, and policymakers is focused on identifying and implementing effective solutions that will help our institutions reach our students. I believe that these solutions will follow from the historical investigation that demonstrates that community colleges, despite their institutional contradictions, are engines of democracy and major contributors to the American marketplace. I also believe that implementing these solutions will be contingent on defining community colleges through their mission statements as places of opportunity, as places where underserved people can achieve great things, and as places where students become thoughtful, productive, empowered citizens.

$\sim$

Although community colleges are critical to the American system of postsecondary education, history has shown the incredible difficulty of aiming for both access and achievement. But of course *difficult* does not mean *impossible*. It is true that under present conditions our institutions cannot be all things to all potential students. However, by working to emphasize individualized attention and enhance academic and student support services, community college leaders, administrators, faculty members, and policymakers can repair the promise we make to the students who depend on us for a way forward.

To implement methods for individualized attention and to enhance academic and student support services, our colleges must comprehensively change, and in some radical ways. Most extensively, our colleges must change the culture in which we operate. At a structural level, this means that our colleges must cease emulating models that do not answer to our institutions' specific needs. First, community college leaders and administrators must cease attempts to reproduce the work of traditional baccalaureate-granting institutions. The numbers cited in Chapter 1 make clear that community colleges and community college students differ radically from traditional postsecondary schools and students. We open our doors to everybody, but because we do, we are responsible for educating students whose academic, financial, and often social needs are frankly incomparable to students at those more traditional postsecondary schools.

Second, while we must cease putting our energy and resources into emulating an institution that does not address the same needs or the same challenges as do our institutions, community college leaders and administrators must also cease efforts to operate as cafeteria-style educational institutions. The cafeteria model took hold at many postsecondary institutions (community colleges and traditional colleges alike) in the 1980s and 1990s, when it was better known as the smorgasbord model. The model was designed to respond to student demands for autonomy and diversity (Smelser & Schudson, 2004). It set new standards for programs, and these standards worked to widen available pathways to award and program completion. The consequence was not just more generous and more adaptable standards but an explosion in course and program offerings.

In its ideal form, the cafeteria model was supposed to create wide institutional appeal by offering incredibly flexible options toward award or program completion. In the real world of community colleges, however, the model translated to an enormous number of courses offered in different vocational-oriented *and* transfer-oriented *and* terminal-oriented *and* continuing education programs. The unprecedentedly large number of courses in an unprecedentedly large number of programs overextended community colleges, overtaxed administrators and faculty members, overwhelmed students, and led, unsurprisingly, to grossly extended times in which students were capable of completing awards and programs.

For students who are unfamiliar with the postsecondary environment or who are the first in their families to attend college—and that describes 36 percent of our learners—the cornucopia of course and program options makes for an overwhelming, to the point of paralyzing, postsecondary experience (AACC 2015 Fact Sheet). Community college students are almost uniformly less prepared for postsecondary coursework than their counterparts at 4-year institutions. The task of navigating hundreds of degree programs and up to thousands of different course options, which would be a difficult task for any student, is especially challenging for *our* students (Bailey, Jaggars, & Jenkins, 2015).

When the institution itself is "fundamentally opaque" (Wyner, 2014, p. 23), students and student support staff feel, and in fact actually are, powerless. Students may strive to find their way, but they often routinely fail in their efforts. Crucially, this is the case for administrators, faculty members, advisors, and other support staff members, too. These college personnel, who are charged with efficiently steering students toward their goals, can be just as bewildered by the innumerable pathways available (or not) to their different students (Bailey, Jaggars, & Jenkins, 2015). Staff and personnel may work to help their students, but they may also lack the extensive knowledge required to determine the most direct or applicable or best way forward. Figuring out how to make progress toward a transfer-oriented outcome, for example, in this "chaotic and confusing environment" can become a nearly impossible task (Wyner, 2014, p. 22). Again, the failure most obviously affects our students, but it also results in real, and negative, institutional data. When students choose courses without fully grasping whether or not the courses will count toward a degree, they significantly delay their chance at graduation and in fact "dramatically reduce [the] likelihood of ever completing a credential" (Wyner, 2014, p. 24).

Certainly, for many institutions there were (and perhaps still are), major benefits associated with the cafeteria model. The model's emphasis on student autonomy privileges self-motivated students who know their path and who are able to capably navigate the obstacles that might block it. The model also allows new students to pick and choose among different courses in an exercise in educational experimentation. The autonomy can help students identify their strengths and weaknesses and can encourage the development of more specific educational goals. But for other students, and particularly for community college students, the autonomy does not result in better, more informed choices. It results in discouraged students who waste extremely limited resources attempting to discern what might eventually prove to be an inaccessible path.

The recent work of Thomas Bailey, Shanna Smith Jaggars, and Davis Jenkins (2015) makes clear that although the cafeteria model *can* provide mostly prepared students with options for filling out the breadth requirements that count toward a baccalaureate degree, for community college students, the cafeteria model just does not work. Over time, its pervasiveness has negatively influenced our institutions and has contributed in major and lasting ways to the persistent poor completion, retention, and transfer rates we see today.

Rather than continue attempts to operate as traditional postsecondary institutions, which simply does not apply to the community college paradigm, and rather than depend on a confounding cafeteria-style array of curricular and program choices, contemporary community colleges' leaders, administrators, faculty members, and policymakers must instead follow the lead outlined by Bailey, Jaggars, and Jenkins (2015). According to their research, community colleges have the best chance of mending the institutional promise to be all things to all potential students by installing comprehensive hands-on support services. I believe that these services must be characterized by excellent academic advisement, thorough and intrusive student support services, effective financial aid interventions, and an extraordinarily prepared faculty that understands, appreciates and celebrates the everyday challenges associated with teaching at a community college.

Bailey, Jaggars, and Jenkins (2015) argue that community colleges can work toward these elements through their guided pathways approach. Such a model is excellent and absolutely necessary, but I believe that our institutions must go even further. To implement a culture of individualized attention and to enhance academic and student support services for our students, community colleges must integrate an institutional culture informed by an *in loco parentis* mandate. This requires a radical shift in community college culture toward meeting the needs of our students, but the shift to a student-centered institution is absolutely necessary to repair our schools and to make the community college promise a reality.

~

My belief in a hands-on, *in loco parentis* community college culture, what I also call a *culture of care* (somewhat after Nell Noddings), is informed by my experience with community college students. Student populations at community colleges are heterogeneous, but they are often united by the fact that for many, entering a community college in the first place is a major achievement.

Many students (probably even most) have overcome any number of obstacles to arrive at our doors. However, the personal, financial, societal, and academic problems that I briefly described in Chapter 1 only scratch the surface of the perniciousness of the issues faced by our students. Too often, we forget that the journey from making the decision to attend community college to completing an award or program is an incredibly difficult, multi-step process that necessitates incomparable persistence on the part of the student and a knowledgeable, efficient, and sympathetic guiding hand on the part of community college faculty members and support staff.

Those of us who have worked in community colleges for even a short amount of time know that for most students, enrollment at community college is not an afterthought. It is instead a serious obligation undertaken after a great deal deliberation. Often, financial status is *the* major point of consideration. This is generally not because of high tuition (although—and crucially—for many students it is). It is instead because enrollment at community college generally means sacrificing both the earnings a student requires to take care of himself or his family and the short-term earning potential he might acquire. The sacrifice requires a careful calculation that weighs an ideally short-term loss against the likelihood of long-term learning opportunities and financial gain, and it strains many students' already incredibly busy and overextended lives.

For many readers, this equation might be relatively easy to solve. But for community college students, the sacrifice, even though it is ideally a short-term one, can be absolutely formidable. To wit, in the colleges I have served, 80 percent to 90 percent of the students who make the decision to enter school qualify for some sort of financial aid. However, only the *most* needy receive financial aid packages that cover tuition and living expenses. The rest of the students, otherwise known as the working poor, do not get the same assistance. They teeter on the poverty line, but they do not have *quite* sufficient need to qualify for full financial aid. These students do not have the relative luxury of enrolling in community college full-time. Or, if they do pursue full-time enrollment, they do so while continuing to work. These are the students for whom making the decision to attend a community college is its own form of achievement.

Of course, however difficult that decision is to make, it is only the first step in a series of similarly difficult decisions. Determining which courses will meet one's abilities, goals, and scheduling requirements, and figuring out how to devise navigable and efficient pathways to achievement via these courses, constitutes the next, often incredibly complicated, step. Too often, this calculation requires too much time and depends too much on a student's intimate knowledge of college-, program-, and course-level logistics. It is no wonder that setting out on a path to completion (particularly a path that will meet students' personal and professional goals) is a hurdle that students with limited time, money, and emotional support simply cannot overcome.

More egregiously, the challenges that students face at this stage can be made far more difficult to navigate by unhelpful community college administrators and staff. I have too often been a witness to the community college culture that neither understands nor helps to accommodate the depth of student need. I specifically remember the case of "Jamie." She came to my office early during my tenure as the Interim President of Bronx Community College.

She was desperate because a delay in her financial aid meant that not only could she not enroll in coursework but that she might also lose her apartment. Despite the apartment's substandard conditions, Jamie was terrified she would lose her home and that she and her 3-year-old would be left to fend for themselves on the street.

Jamie was a victim of domestic violence and a newly single mother. She had completed her first year at BCC and boasted a good grade point average. My office was her last resort. She had already sought help in the bursar's office, but she was advised to drop out because she could not pay the bills. In Jamie's case, dropping out meant more than delaying her graduation. The loss of aid meant a loss of the community college as a structural and social support and, far more immediately, the loss of her home. Not only would dropping out mean that Jamie would *not* be able to continue the work of creating a better life for herself and her child, it would meant that she might not be able to continue any work at all.

I was able to find emergency funds from the Petrie Foundation, a private philanthropic organization, to help Jamie make ends meet until her financial aid check arrived. She was consequently able to survive the crisis and continue her studies. Today, she is actively involved in student governance and on a path to a better life for herself and her family. While Jamie's story ends on a happy note, it is only happy because Jamie possessed a forceful desperation that propelled her to my office. Too often, otherwise successful students are held back by financial difficulties that look a lot like Jamie's. They do not posses Jamie's passion and fearlessness. Even if they did, an impassioned plea to an interim president certainly does not constitute a reliable or implementable solution.

∼

I offer Jamie's story because it sheds light on the dysfunctional culture that pervades so many of our schools. Jamie was not just held back by her financial difficulties, she was held back by an unsympathetic staff uneducated in comprehensive student support and therefore uninterested in her problem. They were ultimately unable and perhaps even unwilling to direct her to a reasonable or reasonably helpful solution. Unfortunately, Jamie's story is not an isolated instance. I have long noted a need for a radical shift in the ways that we in positions of power at community colleges contribute to a culture that does not respect our individual students and that does not work to meet them on their complicated individual paths.

The culture is particularly insidious because it has such deep roots. I remember confronting the same difficulties years ago when I was Dean of Faculty at Middlesex Community College. We had just completed the late-August registration process, and the next day, an agitated middle-aged man suddenly burst into to my office. He was the husband of a potential student, "Alice," and had helped her register the previous day. He wanted me to hear about their experience.

According to his account, Alice entered the registration arena about five minutes before the end of registration. As she approached the faculty member behind the Accounting Major table, she asked if she could register as a freshman in Accounting 101. Her fairly innocuous request was met with a "cackle" of laughter. An insensitive faculty member informed her that the last seat available for Accounting 101 had been filled back in June and that there was no chance that her request would be accommodated. Unprepared for this information, which obviously registered as a blow, Alice lost her courage and walked out.

In my office, her husband was understandably furious. He chastised me and the other administrators and faculty members for failing to consider the mental hardships Alice had had to overcome to walk into that arena at all. Prior to registration, he and Alice sat in the parking lot for three hours as Alice worked up the courage to enter through the college's front doors. She was intimidated by the process: she had never attended college before and had raised her family in a middle-class environment. Now that her children were themselves off to college, she had yearned for the chance to receive a postsecondary education. She had been out of school for so long that she did not believe in her ability to navigate the bureaucracy much less to succeed in the coursework. Her fears transcended the mundane realities of the registration process, but they were treated as trivial.

~

I think that my readers know and agree that we do our students and our institutions a major disservice when we allow their education to be derailed at the bursar's office or during the hoop-jumps and red tape of registration. While we must of course determine substantive solutions to reactively meet the challenges faced by students such as Jamie and Alice, we must also begin to recognize the opportunity to *proactively* intervene in our students' lives before their lives are pushed off course by circumstances that are often outside of their control.

To identify these opportunities requires a radical shift in community college culture toward what I've called a culture of care. It requires all of us associated with community colleges to act as ambassadors of our institutions and to foster an environment in which it is considered unconscionable to turn away students whose needs, while superficially impersonal and unrelated, are in fact intimately tied up in their educational, professional, and life goals.

As I describe above, I consider this culture of care to be inspired by an *in loco parentis* mandate. The invocation of the Latinate is neither condescending nor patronizing, it simply reflects the needs of a critical mass of community college students. To effectively implement a culture of care, community college staff and personnel must adopt an attitude that reflects the community college's promise of access. Simply put, our institutions were founded on welcoming all, and we must embody this welcome. From the college fair, to the bursar's workstation, to the classroom, and in the president's office, we must enable students to see themselves as the rightful inhabitants of the community college's institutional home. If community college leaders, administrators, faculty members, and policymakers are going to meaningfully impact retention, completion, and graduation rates, we must recognize that effective retention strategies begin on the way *in* not on the way *out*. We must match access with a welcoming culture that is firmly in place by the time students make the decision to walk through our doors.

This culture of care is all the more important when considering the large number of our students who enter community college with low self-worth. Just as insidious as financial, academic, and social problems, low self-worth plagues too many community college students, reminding them that they are not good enough for "real" college. Indeed the less-than status that adheres to our institutions is often reinforced by students whose teachers, family members, and even friends have reminded them in various ways that they are not—and never will be—college material. My own grandson was told by an insensitive 5th-grade teacher that he would never graduate from high school because of his inability to do well in math. It seems unbelievable, but he never forgot this. Throughout his life, he struggled with an internalized voice that told him he was not good enough for college-level work. However, quite unlike my many students, my grandson has a supportive network of family and friends who have pushed, pulled, begged, and cajoled him to continue his education at Brooklyn College.

Although our institutions face very real challenges associated with students' poor academic preparation, we cannot meaningfully enhance our students' completion or our institutions' retention rates without attending to student deficiencies that are only peripherally academic. We absolutely need the substantive measures that will allow leaders, administrators, faculty members, and support staff to attend to these deficiencies, but we will go a long way toward developing such measures by first shifting our institutional culture. Embracing the culture of care means making the extraordinary individualized attention required by so many of our students an imperative and not the result of a special situation. Too many of our students come to community college unprepared and insecure: they constitute the majority, *not* the minority of our population. These students need help, but they also need to know that providing that help is part of the community college's institutional promise.

Accordingly, adopting an *in loco parentis* approach means understanding that the circumstances surrounding every one of the applicants to a community college are as varied as the students themselves. Policies that seek to homogenize this heterogeneous group of individuals through blanket support, or that seek superficial bureaucratic fixes for variable, profoundly personal challenges, are doomed to fail. This can be a hard truth for community college leaders and administrators because we often look for procedures that will encompass as many students as possible. While the granularity of our student bodies may make it impossible to establish a broad-brush approach to completion and retention, building and promoting a culture that respects students as individuals and that seeks to solve their individual challenges is a first and essential step to any effective retention program.

~

Of course, for the culture that I advocate to be effective, it must go far beyond attitude and far beyond the level of administration.

It must instead saturate every aspect of our schools. And it must be particularly evident in our classrooms. Administrators can help determine and guide students to an efficient and efficacious path to success, but it is our faculty members who are best positioned to impact and intervene in students' daily lives. The impact and intervention will not happen because of a simple personal change of attitude (although that certainly helps). It happens through the broader, systemic change that recognizes *and* values students with an array of needs as the proper inhabitants of our institutions. Such valuation empowers administrators and faculty members to radically change the community college institutional and classroom environment to reflect the recognition.

It will surprise no one to learn that community college teachers operate under incredibly challenging conditions. However, the extent and intensity of the challenge is seldom the center of the critical conversations about our schools (although I will discuss it more deeply in Chapter 6). The silence is very likely a product of the general unwillingness to candidly describe the challenges our students bring to our schools and our classrooms. It is, as I argue everywhere in this book, a silence that we must break: community colleges and community college students *are* different. Without a clear-eyed accounting of our institution's import and without an honest discussion of the characteristics of the student populations we seek to teach and to serve, we will not be able to transform our institutions into student-centered schools dedicated to facilitating the achievement of all.

Part of this accounting recognizes that community college teachers operate in a completely different environment and must utilize completely different pedagogical strategies than teachers at more traditional postsecondary schools. This is particularly true of research universities. At the risk of oversimplification, the traditional classroom environment (over which most teachers in America are trained to preside) is a competitive environment.

It encourages teachers to weed out students who do not progress beyond fundamentals or who fail to grasp more complicated
concepts despite various presentation and pedagogical strategies.

The pedagogical methods often utilized in this environment
rely on techniques more recognizably rooted in the master-apprentice paradigm of music conservatories and other, similarly traditional institutions. At a conservatory, a talented musician learns
from a master practitioner. The access to mastery encourages
and enables a talented student to thrive. Through hierarchically
based observation, practice, guidance, and critique, an apprentice
musician learns to refine technique and hone the musical craft.
Similarly, at a traditional research university, students often learn
through hierarchically based observation, practice, guidance, and
critique to advance their own knowledge and to discover new
knowledge with the aid of a professor, a recognized master.

Neither the traditional competitive classroom environment
nor the traditional master-apprentice model works at community
colleges. First, the environment plays to our students' persistent
sense of low self-worth. Community college students are incredibly resilient in some surprising contexts, but they are often much
less resilient than other postsecondary students in the context of
the traditional postsecondary classroom. This is often the reason
they seek out the education offered at community colleges. For
students with a history of low or deficient academic performance,
an array of personal challenges, and persistent (if unrecognized)
sense of low self-worth, the traditional classroom environment
can be debilitating. Such students often perceive an initial critical
encounter as validation of their inability to compete. They may
question whether they are wasting money in trying to get an
education or wasting time trying to attend college.

Second, traditional pedagogical methods can fail because
the students at our institutions are often not yet at the level, in
terms of ability (and often in terms of interest) of apprenticeship.

This is particularly the case in the remedial or developmental classroom, where the coursework does not always appear to be immediately applicable to students' future academic goals. The valuable buy-in that implicitly encourages students to continue along the apprenticeship continuum is often off the table before students even have a chance to engage.

That our faculty members work incredibly hard to expand the limits of the community college classroom and diversify their pedagogy is absolutely undeniable. We know that teachers who dedicate themselves to our schools are passionate advocates of community college students. But the academic need in the classroom is often so great that it limits necessary pedagogical experimentation. Faculty members at community colleges must tightly focus their efforts on the speedy delivery of as much useful information as possible. This approach to teaching is as traditional as the master-apprentice model and ironically mimics the traditional pedagogy of the nineteenth century. The irony is particularly keen given that the gentle revolt against the limitedness of this pedagogy indirectly spurred the democratization of postsecondary institutions and the subsequent birth of nascent community colleges.

However, in twenty-first century community colleges, the classical delivery of relevant material is deployed to meet the most immediately obvious need, which in the community college classroom is academic. In fact, despite the varied challenges that community college students bring into the classroom, it is this deep academic need that can strong-arm the pedagogy and all but force faculty members to assume a strictly academically oriented interventionist role. This is not necessarily a reflection of the level of students' unpreparedness; it is instead a reflection of the *critical mass* of students who are academically unprepared. Plainly put, faculty members at community colleges must facilitate learning in classrooms in which the majority of students need a lot of academic help.

This point is not simply based on my own observation. An evaluator of Pedagogy Matters, the faculty enrichment program at LaGuardia Community College noted that "It really cannot be emphasized enough that perhaps no other cohort of instructors in American education confronts such a consistently low-performing group of students on a daily basis" (Mellow & Heelan, 2008, p. 193). At many other postsecondary institutions, faculty members interact with a mixed or more uniformly mid- to high-achieving cohort. The more limited diversity enables the faculty members at these institutions to leverage students' variable abilities to the benefit of all. It also gives faculty members a measure of freedom in which to experiment with different methods for academic delivery.

Faculty members at community colleges rarely have this luxury. First, they must work every day to negotiate learning in classrooms where most students struggle to meet the academic standard. Second, they must also work to help students to reach that standard while attending to students' pervasive financial, social, and emotional needs. Third, they must meet the often-general attitude among community college students that college is necessary but is not necessarily for them. Fourth, they must undertake their work at uniformly underfunded institutions that continue to be marginalized by insiders, such as students, and outsiders, such as high school guidance counselors. At community colleges across the country, faculty members undertake business-as-usual under impossible conditions: they try to engage underprepared, overextended, and unconvinced students in classrooms that do not garner the resources or the respect deserved and needed.

Consequently, at community colleges, faculty members are engaged in an uphill battle in which the hill resembles a mountain. The battle is made all the more difficult because our teachers are seldom trained for this kind of work or for this kind of environment. Instead, our teachers usually undertake the same training as other postsecondary teachers: they learn in an environment that

prepares them for traditional postsecondary schools—which feature a competitive classroom environment—and that favors the
master-apprentice pedagogical style. Given the omnipresent model
for postsecondary schools provided by baccalaureate-granting institutions, the gap in training is a given. It is, however, meaningful:
our teachers must learn the nature of the battle, the slope they
must climb, and the best strategies for navigation while on the job.

Ironically, community college teachers probably have the
most important tasks in our institutions. Unlike most college
leaders and administrators, these faculty members have the relative proximity to students that allows for opportunities for regular
student interactions. Faculty members therefore have the space
necessary and the justification implicitly required to rigorously
interrupt the negative feedback loop that keeps so many students'
perceptions of their academic ability and future worth so low.
Doing so, however, depends on the full integration of a culture
of care at the classroom and pedagogical level. This will not only
provide the appropriate environment but will also equip faculty
members with the tools of supportive individualized intervention. Faculty members must be empowered to build the kinds of
classrooms and individual learning experiences in which students
are encouraged and enabled to view the classroom, and thus the
community college itself, as a safe academic space that will help
them to meet their specific academic and life goals.

Of course, the responsibility makes the already difficult job
of teaching at community colleges even more challenging. A full-
scale cultural shift requires both time and money. More materially,
it requires effective professional development opportunities that
provide faculty members with the support *and* the tools to meet
students' diverse needs. Although community colleges currently
spend very little money providing the type of professional development opportunities that will enable our teachers to effectively
reach our students, given the near majority of adjunct or part-

time faculty at our colleges, professional development is a critical investment in our institutional bottom line.

Student retention depends in no small part on classroom experience: when students feel alienated by community college administrators and by faculty members, they leave. In my experience, they only rarely return. The tremendous financial pressures under which community colleges operate make professional development a luxury, but our institutions must make such development a priority. Only by teaching our leaders, administrators, and faculty members to provide specialized, often individualized teaching and support services will we enact a culture of care that can result in student and institutional success.

Doing so is difficult, but it can be done. I know because throughout my career, I have worked to this end. Community colleges succeed when the particularity of the institution is not just understood but embraced. Community colleges succeed when the particularity of students, who so often arrive with a variety of challenges, are not just tolerated but welcomed. Community colleges succeed when the institution seeks to meet its students through a culture of care made actionable through highly individualized student services. Community colleges succeed only with a great deal of effort and resources, but when the colleges do succeed, the results are extraordinary. The Freshman Academies at Queensborough Community College and the ASAP program at the City University of New York—both of which I describe in the next chapter—demonstrate the positive results of my approach.

I believe that individualized interventions that attend to the whole student are a natural extension of the cultural shift I've described. However, before I turn to the programs that show the institutional rewards of this shift, I must first turn to the community college mission statement. The mission statement might appear a mere philosophical endeavor, far removed from both the day-to-day concerns of a college and its more immediate, pressing issues. But the need to specify what—*exactly*—a community college seeks to offer students and communities reflects the corollary need to clarify for leaders, administrators, faculty members, policymakers, *and* students the directions in which a college should (and seeks to) develop.

We begin the work toward fully implementing a culture of care that privileges individualized learning and student support services when we articulate our values at the most foundational level. By revising our mission statements, we empower our president and trustees to clearly communicate institutional priorities. Through strong mission statements, we enable strong leadership.

Unclear mission statements cannot be blamed for the current crisis faced by our colleges. However, with the help of weak missions, we've promised too much and delivered too little. The mission of every community college should be considered an opportunity to clarify the educational product offered by our colleges and its mode of delivery. The mission should define institutional identity and help direct institutional development. It should act as a covenant with students and stakeholders. Revising and articulating our missions will therefore allow our institutions to redefine and recommit to the twinned promise of access and achievement that we make to our students.

Clearly, the mission statement is tasked with a big job. Unfortunately, it is frequently weak—formulated either too generally or too specifically to be considered meaningful or meaningfully executable. Too-general missions reflect the institution's earliest iteration: just recall the AACC's original description from 1922 situating the junior college as "an institution offering two years of instruction of strictly collegiate grade." The words hardly merit the term "mission," but at the time the colleges depended on it to establish identity and to clarify the educational product offered by the schools. Too-specific missions, which can result from overcorrecting generality, are an outcome of the accountability movement's shift from fad to standard. Whether too general or too specific, weak mission statements force intra-institutional competition and confusion over where and how to most effectively invest time and money (McPhail & McPhail, 2006).

To meaningfully revise mission statements and better enable leaders, administrators, and trustees to articulate the community college promise and better integrate a culture of care, contemporary community college leaders and administrators must work not for generality *or* multiplicity but for *balance*. Leaders and administrators must align a claim to comprehensiveness with narrower focal points that provide substantive, communicative direction. That is to say, a revised institutional mission statement cannot help but account for certain broadness: missions carry major responsibility and community colleges rightly maintain a focus on access. However, the comprehensiveness cannot be so large that it obscures what it attempts to describe. An institution's multiple, potentially conflicting missions may capture the multiple priorities served by community colleges, but they also lend credence to the general suspicion that part of the institution's persistent inability to balance the tension between access and achievement is connected to an institutional tendency to generalize to the point of impossible implementation.

While we must avoid the pitfalls of generality and particularity, we need not avoid the pitfalls of conflict. This may be surprising, but in fact in refining missions to better articulate and ultimately deliver the community college's promise to balance access with achievement, college leaders and administrators must use narrower and more explicit elements and then better manage the conflict that complex missions will certainly breed.

Crucially, our more direct missions should reflect our responsibility to meet, as practically as possible, specific students' needs, our duty to address the requirements of local communities, our commitment to providing America's most qualified global workforce, and our commitment to democracy. New, more relevant community college mission statements will therefore articulate the still-foundational import of access, will prioritize a limited and therefore achievable number of educational goals (both for institutions and for students), and will set out the parameters of a hyperlocally informed relationship to its community.

We know what *should* be done to revise current missions statements in the directions that I describe, but the practical task of creating a meaningful mission statement is far from easy. To create institutional mission statements that are large enough to contain a college's multitudes but not so large as to disable efficient development, community college leaders can turn to the work of Christine Johnson McPhail and Irving Presley McPhail (2006). Johnson and McPhail offer an "operational framework" for leaders and administrators looking to restrict problematic comprehensiveness and eliminate conflict (p. 92). The framework provides a model for asking guided questions about relevance and for gathering data through needs-based assessment to refine institutional aims.

The framework is supremely helpful and can guide the boards of trustees that have taken on an increasingly important role in understanding community needs and in defining the parameters of effectiveness for community colleges. Good mission statements set these types of parameters, and good missions statements can act as templates for other institutions. Anne Arundel Community College in Maryland, for example, communicates a clear mission to its students and its community:

> With learning as its central mission, Anne Arundel
> Community College responds to the needs of a diverse
> community by offering high quality, affordable, and
> accessible learning opportunities and is accountable
> to its stakeholders.

The statement defines the college as a learning institution, engaged in the transmission of knowledge and the advancement of pedagogical research about community college issues. It makes access to students a central theme but establishes the parameters of comparing the educational results with others ("high quality") and provides fiscal accountability ("affordable"). It defines the college's "owners" as the stakeholders, meaning the county funders.

Focused missions that reflect community colleges' core tenets—like open access—and that spell out specific pathways for students—like vocational education—and specific priorities for community relationships—like providing a pipeline for skilled, fairly compensated workers—offer a rudder for community colleges in the uncertain seas of the contemporary postsecondary system. The mission statements at community colleges such as Anne Arundel provide clarity and communication. Ultimately, they help to guide development, help provide students with a clearer vision of progress and achievement, help legitimate our institutional presence, and help enact the community college promise.

Chapter 4

Transformative Interventions

Can We Convert Community Colleges into Student-Centered Institutions?

Thanks to the federal government's belief in the role that community colleges play for the American and global marketplace, our colleges have been increasingly brought from the margins of postsecondary discourse into the mainstream. Unfortunately (although unsurprisingly), our institutions have not necessarily benefited from the attention. Instead, we have been accused of routinely overpromising and under-delivering. Although dead-end institutional and pedagogical models and ineffective mission statements hold back our schools, our institutions are also prohibited from delivering on our promise by unpopular remediation efforts and weak student support services.

Community colleges must therefore enable comprehensive cultural and structural change. We can prepare the environment for this change by first recognizing the singularity of the students we serve and the particular (and particularized) teaching strategies they require to succeed. On the broadest scale, this recognition must be implemented at every level through what I called in the last chapter the culture of care. We can begin the work of activating this culture and enabling it to meet our students' needs by articulating strong mission statements that empower our leaders to develop institutions in particular, and particularly relevant, ways. However, this change is not enough to reinvigorate our schools. We must also turn to the practical work of identifying, creating, and fostering the interventions that will transform our colleges into student-centered institutions.

~

Obviously, our colleges are failing on multiple fronts. It is not just through too-traditional pedagogy and too weak mission statements that we break our promise to our students. Leaders and administrators of community colleges do not currently meet our students' challenges, do not currently provide adequate support for faculty member and teaching support staff, and do not currently comprehensively implement practices that are intimately informed by communities' hyperlocal needs.

Damning data-driven evidence of this contemporary failure may speak more specifically than a historical overview of community colleges' disappointing achievement-related outcomes. The data indicate that community colleges are not only *not* fulfilling their claim to be all things to all *potential* students, but are also *not* adequately educating the *existing* students in their enrollment rosters. Obviously, statistics paint an incomplete picture. The truism is particularly relevant at community colleges because graduation rather than enrollment data are used to determine institutional health. Indeed, the Student-Right-to-Know (SRK) metric, now the most widely used measure of student achievement and the only available metric on graduation and transfer rates for every undergraduate institution in the United States, is particularly problematic.

The SRK metric reports on first-time, full-time students who earn a degree or certificate within 150 percent of the allotted standard time, up to three years for an associate's degree and six years for a baccalaureate degree (Community College Completion, 2015). The data is problematic for nearly all community colleges (Bailey, Crosta, & Jenkins, 2007). First, the information gathered is subject to interpretation: a straight comparison of the definitive *full-time* status, for example, remains unavailable. Second, students who transfer and earn a degree or credential at another institution count as failures because they have failed to complete at the community college they first entered. As many readers well know, because so many community college students transfer and go on to earn credentials elsewhere (although not always in the allotted timeframe), the statistic negatively skews community colleges' performance. Third, despite the success rate associated with full-time student status, most community college students do *not* enroll full-time. The majority of today's students work *and* attend school (and, as we recall, take remedial or developmental courses). Naturally, these students routinely take longer than three years to complete an associate's degree or six years to complete a baccalaureate degree. In fact, they often take much, much longer (Bailey, Crosta, & Jenkins, 2007).

Data like this must be deeply contextualized to be anything other than unrepresentative. Statistics, and most especially comparative statistics, prove consistently problematic for our schools. The colleges and the students the colleges serve are simply too variable to be comfortably grouped within the more homogenous category of traditional 4-year postsecondary schools. While the lack of relevance has been discussed before (Bailey, Calcagno, Jenkins, Leinbach, & Kienz, 2005), it has not always been noted that statistics like these are doubly damaging: they implicitly reinforce community colleges' less-than status but simultaneously encourage community colleges' adoption of the institutional model provided by baccalaureate-granting schools. In the last chapter, I argued that community colleges—and students—are radically different from traditional postsecondary schools. The SRK metric unhelpfully obscures this difference and sets up community colleges in a competition they will always lose.

Despite the fact of incomplete or unrepresentative data, statistics such as those provided by the SRK can and do influence broadly held views. This proved true in the early days of the accountability movement, and it proves true today. Widely reported statistics, such as those indicating that graduation rates sometimes fall below 20 percent, or those that point to retention rates that sometimes fall below 45 percent, paint a picture of community colleges that students, leaders, administrators, policymakers, and the general communities served by the colleges simply do not want to see (U.S. Department of Education, 2014).

But the SRK data do not account for community colleges' promise to enable wide access—to provide a postsecondary education for all potential students. The SRK data do not weight findings to account for the critical mass of community college students whose low academic performance is frequently tied to a host of other challenges. In addition, although the SRK data speak limitedly to community colleges' institutional failures, the data cannot quantify the impact that shattered dreams have on the community college students who drop out. For these students, dropping out often means that the institution has crushed students' last hope for getting ahead.

Certainly, community college leaders and administrators must account for the SRK data and use its findings to better serve our student, teachers, and missions. But leaders and administrators must also candidly recognize the limits of the data. Is modeling the access offered at traditional baccalaureate-granting institutions, and limiting or in some cases denying access, the only way to statistically compete with other institutions and address the plight of our students? Absolutely not. In fact, in the same way we must cease modeling the institutional and pedagogical models of more traditional 4-year schools, we must cease attempting to compete with data that does not always account for profound institutional and student-body variability. We must redefine our institutional and student-body differences as strengths, but we must also recognize that the redefinition cannot come at the cost of the foundation of access on which community colleges are built.

The unfettered access provided by our schools will *always* pose a major obstacle for administrators and educators because it means helping students achieve in a setting for which they are routinely underprepared. And as previous chapters have already shown, most of our students *are* underprepared: 68 percent require remedial coursework. To move forward from a *cri de cœur* for our institutions and students, to identify more effective strategies for improving *our* institutions and for engaging and retaining *our* students, community college leaders and administrators must shift to accommodate not just a new culture and new mission statements, but new models for remediation and student support.

The need for new models is possibly nowhere more acute than in the arena of remediation and other, often related interventionist student support. While a mission can lay out the terms for achievement, remediation and student support services go the distance in making achievement a real possibility, particularly for underserved minority students, students with limited educational success, and students with limited postsecondary experience.

According to the AACC's 2015 Fact Sheet, these descriptors fit the majority of our students. In the fall of 2013, community college undergraduates accounted for 57 percent of the nation's Hispanic undergraduates, 52 percent of its African American undergraduates, 61 percent of its Native American undergraduates, and 43 percent of its Asian/Pacific Islander undergraduates.

Additionally, community colleges offered access to postsecondary education to over 40 percent of undergraduates living in poverty (Mullin, 2012). And this last data point does not even include the population I referred to as the working poor in Chapter 3.

As I've argued, because community colleges offer these previously disenfranchised students an opportunity to experience higher education, the institution must be capable of responding to their needs. Unprepared students predictably require the most intensive student support. Unfortunately, what un- or underprepared students too often receive is academic support in the form of ineffective remedial coursework. Remediation is theoretically crucial to incoming students' success, but remediation in practice is unevenly integrated at the institutional level and bears too little (or too oblique) a relationship to college-level courses. In fact, remediation seldom outlines a logical or even clear pathway to more substantive, credit-bearing programs (Safran & Visher, 2010).

When the majority of incoming students are identified as in need of some sort of intensive academic support services, and when those services take the form of non-integrated remediation, community colleges have already begun to break the institutional promise to provide all students a reasonable pathway to achievement and success. In this context, delivering on our larger institutional promise is totally overwhelming—among other things, it requires our administrators, teachers, and support staff to correct years of academic deficiencies in a finite period of time with classes that are not necessarily clearly connected to future academic coursework. We can better situate our institutions to respond to students' deficiencies by redefining those deficiencies beyond the academic: to provide a more practical but also more meaningful response to student need, community college leaders, administrators, teachers, and support staff must combine remediation and pedagogical intervention with broadly integrated student support services.

Cohen, Brawer, and Kisker (2013) have pointed out that remedial education is a core competency at community colleges. In fact, I believe that the contemporary profile of the student need at community colleges means that remedial coursework must in fact be considered a *primary* offering on community college campuses. This is an important recognition. In my experience, community college leaders and administrators tend to view remediation as an unnecessary drain on institutions' fiscal resources. At the same time, faculty members and students tend to view remediation as validation that community college students are not college material. Community college leaders, administrators, faculty members, *and* students must work toward recognizing remediation (and not just remedial coursework) as the structural bulwark deeply intertwined with an effective, rigorous community college curriculum.

In fact, productive, integrated remediation has almost always been a contingency of institutional open access. In 1970, when the City University of New York established an open admissions policy for all its units, the administrators, faculty members, and community members were skeptical. They questioned how standards could be maintained when everyone with a high school diploma could gain admittance. Understandably, administration, faculty members, and others initially assumed the policy would throw an insurmountable obstacle in the way of success. They saw the policy as flawed and assumed that the increase in access would negatively impact the ability of faculty members to impose exacting rigor to the curriculum.

Happily, not everyone shared this view. Mina Shaughnessy, in particular, believed that with additional help and specialized programs an open admissions policy could work to the benefit of all students. Shaughnessy had worked at the City College since 1967 as Director of Search for Education, Elevation, and Knowledge (SEEK). She also had extensive experience with teaching writing to underprepared students. She therefore knew quite clearly of what she spoke. When the CUNY Board of Trustees adopted the open admissions policy in 1970, her program mushroomed. In response to the need, Shaughnessy developed a graduate-level course in composition to teach the SEEK program to writing instructors and made frequent presentations to other units of the university (Maher, 1997; Shaughnessy, 1977). In 1977, Shaughnessy published *Errors and Expectations: A Guide for the Teacher of Basic Writing*. Her book, which laid out a basic approach to remediation, was an instant success because it indicated that an egalitarian approach to admissions did not necessarily result in a dilution of standards.

Shaughnessy's thesis that open access *need not* depress academic standards was revolutionary at the time. Today, however, while her argument still holds sway, it is no longer *practically* true. Its inapplicability does not reflect the strength of the argument; it reflects the growth of community colleges. To revive Shaughnessy's emphasis on effective remediation in an age in which community colleges house many more and a much needier student population, demands significant contemporary reforms. This is particularly true because, since the initial days of the CUNY Board of Trustees' decision to formally open admissions at all levels of the university system, research has furthered our understanding of the ways that current methodology for developmental education impacts students.

Research conducted by the CCRC suggests that, for the most part, the traditional system of developmental education is not realizing its intended purpose (Bailey & Cho, 2010). The results reflect the incredible difficulty of successfully remediating twelve years of bad study habits, financial and social challenges, and low self-worth in one, two, or three semesters. In my experience, students with remedial needs in one area (in reading, writing, or computational skills, for example) can benefit from the additional help offered by remedial courses. However, for students with deficiencies in two or three areas, the rate of success as defined by retention dwindles (Attewell, Lavin, Domina, & Levey, 2006). Even at CUNY, the graduation rate of students who place into remediation is far lower after six years than those who do not have remedial needs: 26.1 percent to 40.3 percent (CUNY Working Group on Remediation, 2011).

Remediation poses a particular problem for contemporary community colleges because its institutional development is susceptible to the application of less funded, less researched, less effective, and less longstanding programmatic solutions. These problems are partly the result of the diffuse and still somewhat disorganized community college system; they are also the result of the fact that the creation and delivery of remedial work is particular to the college. Remediation, often quite unlike other programs, is critically informed by an array of factors, including area high schools, student demographics, university and employer expectations, accreditation requirements, and institution-specific accountability measures such as placement exams (Kazeracki & Brooks, 2006). Consequently, each college develops in-situ remediation designed to meet the needs of its specific students. Despite the fact that all our schools welcome student populations with difficult-to-tally and difficult-to-meet remediation needs, we cannot always learn from each other what works best because the populations are so different.

While student need should dictate both the place of remedial or developmental education at an institution and its relative import, that is not always the case. We already know that students' need are great, but as in so much else, we also know that effective execution is often wanting. In fact, many leaders, administrators, and faculty members are all too aware that despite intense effort over the past decades (Bailey, 2009), developmental education functions incompletely and inadequately (Hughes & Scott-Clayton, 2011). As a result, far too few of our students who engage in remedial or developmental coursework are able to successfully transition to higher-level courses, much less program or award completion (Kozeracki & Brooks, 2006).

To illustrate the complexity of the problem, consider, for example, high school graduates who enter community colleges with below grade-level mathematics skills. These students are deficient in mathematics, but simple deficiency is not the whole story. Instead the story begins back in 9th grade (and often even earlier), when these students first began to fall behind. For various reasons, the students fell behind in mathematics skills and failed to catch up. Maybe they slipped through the net of accountability because they were able to avoid mathematics classes in 11th and 12th grade. Whatever the reason, the depth of their need remained unrecognized throughout their secondary education, and their skills remained unpracticed. By the time these students arrive at community colleges, they have been out of any similar practice for at least the last three years. The students must then take a placement exam to determine their skill level. It should surprise no one that few of these students score sufficiently high in the exams to enter *any* college-level math course.

The task of providing effective remediation for these particular students is incredibly difficult, and they represent only a fraction of the need faced by so many community colleges. Often, only those students who are extremely motivated or who have the natural ability to do well will succeed. Of course, the majority of students take remedial courses because they lack one or the other (and sometimes both). In my experience, most students navigate remedial requirements by either dropping out or by repeating courses until they are able to meet the standards. If they drop out, they fall behind even further—and often permanently. If they stay and repeat coursework, they chew up their financial aid eligibility. When these students finally exit from remediation and complete an associate's degree, they often find that they have run out of money before they can complete a baccalaureate degree. This is self-selection at its draconian worst.

Community college leaders and administrators face further challenges, as well. When Shaughnessy developed her approach to responding to the widespread need for efficient remediation, community colleges did not account for nearly as many undergraduates nor did they boast quite as many diverse students. "Diversity" itself also had a more limited meaning. Our students are not just ethnically diverse, but diverse in education, professional experience, financial, and social challenges. Forty-five years after Shaughnessy's efforts, the students who matriculate at community colleges need remediation services that are as variable as *they* are.

Unfortunately, community colleges are often thwarted in their efforts to create these more individualized approaches by the very placement exams that determine the need for remediation. The exams do not often account for a plethora of applied skills, for example, skills that often include mathematics. The exams are also usually too general and are usually incapable of functioning as a meaningful diagnostic tool. Instead, the exams simply indicate whether or not a student's skills are commensurate with her peers and her grade level. The data provided by the exams encourage a one-size-fits-all approach that leaves support staff and faculty members without the necessary information for matching students to the most appropriate interventions.

The case for more comprehensive, more connected, and thus more effective remediation has been building, particularly in the last decade, thanks to research conducted at the Community College Research Center (CCRC) (Hodara, Jaggars, & Karp, 2012;

Visher et al., 2012). However, the difficult task of determining the most effective developmental education has not yet received nearly enough research attention. Of course, both research and the implementation of research necessitate funding, and the high cost of remedial and developmental programs is already staggering. By some accounts, remedial services at community colleges range from 1.9 to 2.3 billion dollars (Strong American Schools, 2008).

In the past, academic administrators worked to keep the institutional costs of remediation down by relying on new or part-time faculty to teach remedial courses. Although asking teachers with less experience to teach the colleges' neediest students is often a faulty, and in its own way, costly model, these new teachers have been responsible for an important shift. In fact, thanks in part to the influx at community colleges of young, committed faculty members who value teaching and research equally, a great deal more attention has begun to be paid to the import of remediation and developmental education.

Over the last five to ten years, I have seen many bright doctoral candidates elect to teach at community colleges over more prestigious 4-year institutions. These teacher-scholars are often attracted, like I was so many years ago, to our institution's democratic ideals and to our willingness to work toward the practical achievement of all potential students. Sometimes, these candidates hear the federal government's call that community colleges constitute America's future; sometimes, they are enticed by the difficulty of the colleges' deep and seemingly intransigent problems. Whatever the reason, these teachers and scholars feel called to contribute to the body of knowledge emerging around best practices in remediation and developmental education. I wholeheartedly welcome this trend, even when it points to problems and even when it calls for more comprehensive change and yet more funding. The passion and work of these teachers and researchers infuses our sector with excitement for engaging in serious examination of how best to reach and teach our students.

Various examples of the results of this shift already show promise. Places like the Community College of Baltimore County (CCBC) in Maryland, for example, have experimented with the Accelerated Learning Program, or ALP. ALP allows some students to bypass remediation in favor of taking modified college-level coursework. When the program allowed students whose placement-exam results fell just below the cutoff scores for remediation to take English 101 with an additional hour of extra support, those students excelled. According to research conducted by CCRC, students receiving this type of treatment did just as well as those students who were placed in Freshman English remediation (Jenkins, Speroni, Belfield, Jaggars, & Edgecombe, 2010).

The current efforts developed by the Washington State Board for Community and Technical Colleges also show promise. Unlike the approach at CCBC, Washington's model is more interventionist and integrated, and thus more along the lines of my own argument. The model, called Integrated Basic Education and Skills Training (I-BEST), is designed to reach students who would otherwise merit non-integrated remedial courses. In I-BEST, such students take courses developed and taught by co-instructors. An occupational or technical instructor and a basic-skills instructor work together to integrate basic skills-level pedagogy into college-level occupational or technical coursework. The paired approach provides students with an integrated on-ramp to college-level courses. As students progress through the program, they learn basic skills in real-world scenarios offered by the college and career portion of the curriculum (Wachen, Jenkins, & Van Noy, 2011).

Another positive development in integrated remediation, which began at City University of New York, is CUNY Start. The program responds to the premise that remedial courses too often serve as a barrier rather than a safety net. The premise is well informed. In 2010, 78 percent of all community college students entering the City University of New York required remediation in reading, writing, or computational ability. Of these students, 23.8 percent required all remediation in all three areas (CUNY Working Group on Remediation, 2011). Students with needs in three remedial areas are at a very high risk of dropping out. In fact, at Queensborough Community College, we found that only 5 percent of students with three remedial deficiencies graduated in 6 years.

Based in part on these dismal statistics, the City University of New York inaugurated CUNY Start as a way forward for students with broad remedial needs. CUNY Start provides intensive preparation in academic reading/writing, math, and "college success." The program enrolls prospective CUNY students who have a high school or high school equivalency diploma, who are not yet ready for college-level work according to the CUNY assessment tests. The program's most attractive feature, aside from the comprehensive safety net it seeks to provide, is its preservation of students' financial aid. Because it is delivered through the continuing education arm of the university system, the program is offered at a very low cost of $75 per semester. Subsequently, students do not have to pay regular tuition, and they preserve their financial aid eligibility when it can more meaningfully contribute to an associate degree or to future baccalaureate work.

∼

While efforts to implement more comprehensive solutions have found a footing at many community colleges and have been able to contribute to the success of students, not all efforts are met with welcome. This has been the case at Bronx Community College (BCC) in response to the Statway and Quantway models of remediation. The models were developed by the Carnegie Foundation for the Advancement of Teaching in 2010. The foundation created a network of colleges to examine and then reform developmental math sequences. The network and the associated initiative resulted in the Statway and Quantway accelerated courses. Statway combines college-level statistics with developmental mathematics and delivers courses focused on statistics, data analysis, and causal reasoning. Quantway, which offers quantitative reasoning coursework, fulfills developmental requirements but also aims to prepare students for success in college-level mathematics. Both methods work to reduce the amount of time it takes students at the basic-skills level to begin engaging in college-level coursework and earning college-level credits.

So far, the reported results have been impressive. According to a report by Sowers and Yamada (2015), a traditional remedial pathway in mathematics resulted in a 6 percent success rate, but for students enrolled in Statway courses, 49 percent completed the remedial course with a grade of C or better. For Quantway, the results were even more significant: after one semester in Quantway courses, students' success rates jumped to 56 percent as compared to a rate of 29 percent for students engaged in traditional remedial curriculum.

Perhaps surprisingly, institutions have been somewhat slow to adopt these programs. Forty-nine institutions in 14 states have integrated the Statway and Quantway remedial mathematics delivery model into their coursework. The slow uptake is informative because it reflects some of the difficulties in adoption and implementation. In my own university system, for example, only two of seven community colleges have adopted the program models. The reluctance indicates both the paucity of uniformly positive research and the subsequent inability of leaders, administrators, faculty members, and student support staff to agree on effective approaches.

Such inability, while understandable, can completely disable the overhaul required to implement more effective support services. At Bronx Community College, for example, the mathematics department faculty insists that students complete the college algebra requirement before graduation. This is a major obstacle for many students. In many instances, students have completed all of the requirements for graduation except the algebra requirement. The issue is certainly not a stubborn faculty. In fact, the faculty members are absolutely well intentioned: they hold tutorial sessions for students and work hard to provide students with the additional instruction required.

Although the broader university administration wants all of its community colleges to integrate the Statway and Quantway model into their classrooms, many members of the BCC faculty, to take just one college as an example, believe that the program dilutes curriculum standards. The faculty members are simply unwilling to adopt a different and in many ways untested model. Unlike in the earlier days of attempts to implement more comprehensive remediation, this kind of conflict will not be resolved until more research concerning the best possible remedial approaches is conducted. In the meantime, the people who suffer the most are the students.

The above example hints at some of the obstacles that stand in the way of the comprehensive implementation and efficient delivery of developmental education. Much of the difficulty depends on complicated issues surrounding student need and incomplete research on pedagogy, and colleges do themselves no favors by requiring students to take ineffective assessment exams. Designed as indicated above, to identify students with academic deficiencies, the exams too often rely on hard cutoffs and place students in remedial courses when they can in fact succeed at college-level coursework (Scott-Clayton, Crosta, & Belfield, 2014). The exams therefore contribute to an already haphazard system that stands in place of other, more intensive, and more direct and applicable interventions that can ideally give students pointed support in their nascent postsecondary careers (Engstrom & Tinto, 2010). To better, more efficiently, and more economically meet the deep need for remediation, the assessments tests must be fine-tuned.

Additionally, and more broadly, leaders, administrators, faculty members, and students alike must accept remedial courses and developmental education as a piece of the extensive support offered by our institutions (and promised by our missions). In fact, I believe that adoption and integration depends on embracing remedial services and developmental education as the very *foundation* of the culture of care and its associated interventional support. Rather than viewing developmental education as a nongenerative drain on resources, a necessary evil, or a byway that thwarts student progress, we must activate an attitude on our campuses that reflects a belief in remediation as a manifestation of the culture of care and as the type of assistance from which the *majority* of our students can benefit.

Consequently, our schools cannot simply adopt or haphazardly integrate developmental education; we must enable excellent, *comprehensive* execution. This does not mean that developmental education must be fully and intimately connected to every program in a community college, but it does mean that remedial education cannot be *isolated* from other programs. The segregation, so common at so many schools, creates too many barriers for students by structurally reinforcing the already major obstructions standing in the way of a ramp onto college-level coursework (Kozeracki & Brooks, 2006). Rather than cordoning off the faculty for remedial education courses from other courses and programs, we must strive instead to implement a *pervasive* remedial culture whereby all participants in community colleges recognize, accept, and welcome remediation as a part of every classroom, not just the classroom specially designated as remedial. Indeed, in my experience, the kind of ad-hoc remediation that happens outside the remedial classroom can sometimes be the most effective, and can better equip our students to reach their goals.

When community college courses do not provide meaningful intervention and support—when they do not direct students onto paths that might lead to higher achievement—they fail students, but they fail communities, too. Remedial education deserves our focus because the stakes are high. They're high in regards to student and institutional performance, and they're high in regards to resource disbursement. Plus, remedial education is here to stay. In the post-Shaughnessy era, this should go without saying, but the contemporary profiles of student need suggest that remedial education is more necessary today than it has ever been.

Because of its importance, remediation must be addressed as a complex educational problem that merits both comprehensive and deep research efforts. The need for coordinated innovation is great. The trends in teaching, in research, and in the initiatives and programs that I cite above show a way forward, but as of yet, the way seems disconnected and chaotic. This is the case even within the programs themselves (Wachen, Jenkins, & Van Noy, 2011). However, and like so much else connected to community colleges, although remediation presents a particular challenge in terms of coordination, it also presents an opportunity. Through the serious pedagogical research that is already being undertaken, we will determine the best diagnostic tools and the best prescriptions to ameliorate our students'—and our institutions'—complicated issues.

～

Of course, remediation is but one area of support required by our students. Notwithstanding the complexity of poor academic preparation, to enhance completion rates for community college students, we need to look beyond remediation or deficiencies that are usually too strictly labeled academic. As I've vehemently argued, students arrive at community colleges with a variety of challenges that may be only peripherally related to academic challenges. In fact, many students arrive at community colleges with absolutely no academic deficiencies. The assessment exams, while far too general, do at least succeed in telling us that these students are ready for college-level work.

Ironically, this report of readiness is another way in which the assessment exams are not always a useful tool. Often, the challenges faced by our students have nothing to do with academics, and these challenges frequently prove the most difficult to solve. They are hard for standardized tests to quantify or describe, and are often the ones that stand most firmly in the way of academic success. To take but one example, many students arrive at community colleges without understanding or fully grasping the long, sequential (but not always clearly or obviously sequential) progression required to achieve an academic goal. This misunderstanding is only peripherally related to academics, but it is one of the major impediments to community college students' success. To respond to these types of uncategorizable shortcomings, it is imperative that community college students are given extraordinary individualized attention upon entry.

∽

The great majority of community college students enter community colleges looking for a better way, a pathway to the middle-class. As I argued in Chapter 3, even though tuition costs are relatively low, for students who are dependent on work and who have family responsibilities, the time constraints, the impact of lost wages, and the tuition costs together make college attendance a very serious commitment. It is hard to imagine a student coming to a community college who is not sincere about attaining an education. What sometimes prevents us from understanding the complexity of these students' needs is that many students seem to come to us with a chip on their shoulder. They are afraid of facing another potentially closed avenue to achievement. They require, I believe, excellent entry-level services to shrug off troublesome pasts and move forward.

Excellent execution of entry-level services begins with appropriate student placement. We must stop relying on the general assessment tests, which immediately challenge students' self-worth and which often contribute to the problem of misplacing students in classrooms where they quickly become unchallenged and uninterested. We must instead refine our criteria for identifying the students who can succeed in college-level coursework and the students who require modifications. Thorough vetting for placement necessitates defining the skills necessary for college success *away* from one test for academic skills and *toward* a holistic approach that accounts for the other skills that can also signal postsecondary success, such as practical skills gained through professional or personal experience (Bailey, 2009; Bailey, Jaggars, & Jenkins 2015; Robbins et al., 2004; Scott-Clayton, 2011). More thorough evaluations require an initial investment in time and resources, but it is by far more efficient and budget-oriented than putting students in remedial coursework where their interest and ability wither and die.

Excellent execution of entry-level services also begins with front-end individualized attention to student goals. Entry-level academic advisement and personal counseling is absolutely imperative to success. Entry-level advisors have to be savvy about student behavior, understanding what might be a mask of bravado and what might indicate closely held goals; they have to be good at interviewing students; they have to be able to make a thorough diagnostic assessment of academic, social, and financial needs; and they must be familiar with the curricular offerings of the college and the college's ability to provide the services that each student needs.

Every student who enters community college must be able to make use of this deeply informed advisement staff. In fact, each entering student should be assigned to an advisor, a coach, or similarly positioned administrator who can help with navigating both the community college experience and the community college as an institution. The advising contact should establish an initial meeting with each incoming student to discuss the student's academic, professional, and personal goals. We often find that underprepared students have unrealistic aims that are frequently informed by a mistaken notion of academic progression and procurement. An advisor can ensure that students are able to articulate their dreams but that such discussions actually inform a realistic plan and a navigable pathway to achievement. The plan and pathway should include an explicit clarification of the student's goals, and it should be obvious to both student and advisor how each step of the plan contributes to reaching the student's desired outcome.

Clearly, this process depends on the individual clarification of goals that will enable advisor *and* student to create a reasonable academic pathway to achievement. The individualization of the service is critical. As the current status of achievement at our institutions makes clear and as recent research corroborates (Bailey, Jaggars, & Jenkins, 2015), community colleges cannot offer *either* a too basic, one-size-fits-all approach *or* a too-complicated cafeteria approach, and expect students to achieve their aims. The promise our institutions make when we welcome all students is a promise to provide *each* student a path by which to achieve professional and personal ambitions. Individualized entry-level services, which include thorough, holistic assessment and personal advising services enable colleges to make good on this covenant.

Once the student and advisor together provide a prescription, the rest of the process depends on monitoring student progress through periodic check-ins and determining that each student is able to access the support services necessary to meet goals. This entry-level process is incredibly, undeniably hands-on and engaged, but some colleges are already effectively providing it and are able to demonstrate dramatic results.

One of the most effective entry-level programs for student support to appear in recent years is the Accelerated Study in Associate Degrees Program (ASAP). Developed at the City University of New York in the fall of 2007 with resources from the New York City Center for Economic Opportunity, ASAP was developed to improve the graduation rates and thus the economic futures of its participants. The initiative started with the lofty goal of graduating at least 50 percent of students within three years. It uses four connected elements to reach this aim: first, it works to radically decrease the financial barriers faced by students in their pursuit of full-time study; second, it offers incredibly comprehensive student support services; third, it provides a highly structured pathway through coursework that includes clearly articulated expectations for students; and fourth, its programs work within a deeply interconnected community of students and staff.

According to most measures, ASAP is a raging success (Scrivener, Weiss, Ratledge, Rudd, Sommo, & Fresques, 2015) and is widely hailed as an excellent model for enabling student completion and graduation (Fain, 2015). In its first year of implementation it already showed incredible promise: 55 percent of the fall 2007 cohort earned their associate degrees within three years (versus 24.7 percent of a group of similar students). Further analysis of subsequent cohorts indicate that ASAP students have stronger retention rates, pass through remedial coursework and associated requirements more quickly, and secure degrees at a higher rate than other students (Scrivener, Weiss, Ratledge, Rudd, Sommo, & Fresques, 2015). Surprising many, the program is also cost-effective. While ASAP requires a significant outlay for participating students, it ultimately saves institutions money by raising retention and graduation rates (Levin & Garcia, 2012). The program is now implemented at nine CUNY schools and aims to serve over 13,000 students by 2017.

While the ASAP program offers a beacon of promise, it has not yet been systematically or comprehensively integrated or integrated at enough institutions. Guttman Community College, formerly the New Community College at CUNY, stands as an important exception. The college, which is founded on many ASAP elements, opened after two years of intensive examination of the existing advances in community college education. Based on the finding that community college students are more likely to achieve their aims if they enroll full-time—a finding also leveraged by ASAP—GCC requires all students to attend on a full-time basis. In fact, all students must commit to attending the college for 22 hours per week. To help students navigate the major commitment they make to the college, GCC provides an extraordinary array of academic and student support services during the entry-level process.

Guttman Community College's curriculum is based on five key principles: providing a first-year curriculum that requires full-time attendance for all students; infusing what is typically defined as remedial education into credit-bearing coursework; offering a limited number of carefully chosen majors; providing proactive academic advisement and counseling; and staffing highly specialized, actively collaborative faculty members. The principles manifest in meaningful action. For example, the faculty members teach a one-year course, Ethnographies of Work (EOW), that combines anthropology and sociology to examine different types of work and workplaces. In addition, a Partnership Office works with the faculty, staff, and administration to develop and sustain relationships with industry, employers, community organizations, and government agencies for purposes of curriculum planning, developing internship, and employment opportunities.

Although GCC has only been operating for three years, early results are encouraging: its retention rate in fall of 2013 was 69 percent, and its 2-year graduation rate for its fall 2012 cohort was 28 percent (guttman.cuny.edu). Clearly, the comprehensive and systemic model provided by GCC is not for every student or for every community. But it works particularly well in New York City as part of the City University of New York, perhaps because students frequently see community colleges as platforms to baccalaureate-granting institutions. For communities that are more interested and invested in developing a well-trained workforce, however, only particular and particularly applicable elements of this model may be appropriate.

~

A program that enables these community colleges to implement some of the most important aspects of the ASAP and Guttman model is the Freshman Academies that I helped implement at Queensborough Community College. This successful initiative offers yet another example of a successful approach to providing effective, intensive student support services. The program was designed by faculty and leaders to give full-time freshmen a jump-start on their path to achievement. To that end, all incoming full-time freshmen receive individualized attention as they earn their first 24 credits. Part of the individualized attention is the result of the placement of each full-time freshman into one of five academies. The academies reflect students' broad goals and include the Business Academy, the Liberal Arts Academy, the Health Related Sciences Academy, STEM, and Visual and Performing Arts.

Each academy houses coordinators who serve as ombudspersons for the incoming students. The coordinators communicate with academic advisors, with counselors, and with faculty members to create an individualized academic plan for each student. The coordinators then follow students' progress, receiving reports from faculty members regarding excessive absences or unexpectedly low grades. The coordinators continue meeting with their students, both formally and informally in the academy's offices, providing "high-impact activities" designed to create cohorts of students around common interests. In this manner, students engage in less formal academic cohorts through joint participation in group projects. In large part, the success of the program has only been met through the centralized and entry-level advisement center. The college hired 10 advisors to assist the process of program development, and the advisors have been able to supply students with the support they need to succeed.

Freshmen Academies, which leaders and faculty members at Queensborough initially offered as a kind of experiment, has been comprehensively successful. The retention and graduation rate at the college is among the highest in the City University system, and students routinely report satisfaction with their experience there. The program was deemed so valuable to students that my successor to the college presidency has expanded the program to include all students during their stay at the college.

To my mind, one of the most crucial components of the success of Queensborough's Freshmen Academies was the fact that leaders, administrators, and faculty members generated the program *together*. Before the Freshmen Academies were developed, many CUNY leaders, administrators, and faculty members were engaged in intense discussions about how to strengthen retention, graduation, and student satisfaction within our colleges. Most of the approaches centered on the ASAP program. Queensborough leaders, administrators, and faculty members were inspired by the approach and wanted to respond to the call to find new ways to impact the rates that consistently lagged at our own college. What resulted from the joint discussions was the Freshman Academies.

The importance of ensuring that every sector at Queensborough Community College—from its leaders to its faculty members to the wider community—had a stake in its development cannot be overstated. Only by working together, were our leaders, administrators, and faculty members able to create a *meaningful*, comprehensive program that continues to positively impact student achievement.

≈

As interim president of Bronx Community College, I worked to put into practice many of the elements of successful program development—including entry-level student support and programs developed jointly by administrators and faculty members—that I learned at Queensborough. Unlike Queensborough, however, Bronx Community College is a much more traditional college. It is housed in a beautiful campus in the Bronx with a strong, traditional-university feel. Built in 1898 as the uptown campus for New York University, BCC houses 39 buildings on 43 acres. Its faculty's academic preparation, which is informed by the college's deep roots, is extraordinarily high. In part, it is informed by the City University of New York requirement that incoming assistant professors hold a PhD. These qualifications, which mirror a more traditional 4-year setting, ensures that faculty members have deep research capabilities and a culture that values continuous engagement with college and student-centered activities.

Bronx Community College, similar to Guttman Community College, offers an exciting case study for the future development of community colleges in the direction of increased student support. While the college seems modeled in the mold set by more traditional 4-year colleges, contemporary pressures have challenged this approach and have worked to produce important student-centered initiatives. Happily, the college and its leaders, administrators, and faculty members are deeply committed both to research and to integrating new pedagogical approaches into their classrooms and have largely embraced the changes. For example, a very active group of researchers and teachers regularly come together as part of the Center for Excellence in Teaching and Learning to engage in substantive discussion about community college pedagogy. In addition, the administrators, leaders, advisors, and faculty members continue to work together to ensure that BCC's ASAP program is one of the best and strongest performing in the City University of New York system.

In fact, because of the enthusiasm of the faculty and because of the current Chancellor's track record with the ASAP program, the Chancellor has been able to obtain 42 million dollars from the City of New York to significantly expand ASAP. The expansion will allow the program to expand from 4,000 students to 25,000 students. As of the fall of 2016, *all* full-time students attending Bronx Community College will be part of the ASAP program. According to early progress reports, we expect the current full-time-student 3-year graduation rate of 11 percent to increase to over 50 percent.

Of course, the college has much to do to meet this goal. Because so much of the program depends on the continuation and intensification of support services, BCC must quickly implement on-the-ground strategies for the individualized support services required for community college student success. For instance, the college must significantly revamp the entry-level advisement process and include services that address students' financial and social needs; the college must continue efforts to establish a strong department of success coaches who are able to monitor the progress of every full-time student; the college must also continue to engage faculty in the development of curricula that are compatible with the ASAP program.

The money available to expand ASAP represents an exciting opportunity for Bronx Community College. It also represents an exciting opportunity for other community colleges, whose leaders, administrators, and faculty members will likely look to BCC as a new institutional model for success. Of course, the opportunity is contingent on the responsibility to meet very ambitious goals regarding retention, completion, and graduation. If BCC's faculty and administration are successful in converting what is at heart a more traditional college into an effective contemporary institution that not only provides students with unfettered access to postsecondary school but also ensures extraordinary completion rates, BCC will become a laboratory for other community college leaders, administrators, faculty members, and support staff.

～

Ultimately, to continue to enlarge upon its success with ASAP, Bronx Community College must develop its support services along specific lines. It must, for example, integrate methods for the continuous monitoring of student progress. Intensive advisement cannot fall off once students are enrolled in their first community college semester. Rather, students benefit from a consistent monitoring mechanism that gauges their academic progress. As I've continued to argue, community college students' lives are complicated, and many students are financially and sometimes socially vulnerable. Sometimes, the slightest glitch in their lives can significantly impact academic progress. It is therefore imperative for colleges to maintain constant vigilance so as to handle potential distractions that may cause students to fall behind.

This type of "constant vigilance" is also described, and often in relationship to ASAP, as *intrusive* intervention. Intrusive intervention is the type of advisement I've already described—it is intervention managed not by one advisor but by an academic team. The team often consists of a success coach, a faculty member, a member of the student services or student support staff, and other members of the college community as their participation is deemed necessary. The most effective methods for intrusive intervention divide responsibilities: the success coach is the team's point person; the faculty member is in control of the academic content and the rigor of the student's curriculum; the student services or student support staff member monitors nonacademic challenges. Each member of the academic team also takes on other responsibilities. The faculty member is engaged in monitoring students' response to classroom activities, and other academic team members note and communicate changes in behavior or performance.

Successful intrusive intervention gives faculty members the power to trigger the formation and involvement of an academic team. Once an academic team is activated on behalf of the student, the existing resources of the college are often placed at the team's disposal. For example, if a faculty member asks that an academic team form to intervene with a student with psychological or social difficulties, then the counseling department becomes involved as part of the student's academic team. If a faculty member forms an academic team because of a student's emergent financial problems, then members of the administration join the academic team, intervening by accessing resources via private philanthropy or federal or state resources. If a faculty member engages an academic team to aid a student with academic concerns, tutors become part of the team. If a faculty member is concerned with a student's time management skills or study habits, a success coach works with the student to access existing resources.

Crucially, the team approach to student success places the responsibility for retention on the *college* rather than on the student. While the intervention is absolutely obtrusive, it is designed to intervene on behalf of students who struggle the most. In that sense, it is not appropriate for all students; it is, however, quite appropriate for many. By creating an academic team that assists the most vulnerable students through their community college experience, the institution fulfills its promise to build a path to achievement for all students who have been accepted.

Taking a proactive stance in retaining these students ensures that the community college provides an individualized service similar to what is provided at many private schools. This can be very beneficial. The extra attention signals to the student that their success is important to the school and to the community the school seeks to serve. In my experience, when this kind of intensive intervention is successful, students come to realize that an entire community is behind them and that the community, through their taxes, has provided the resources necessary for students' success. The transition toward seeing resources as an *entitlement to scholarship* is important. Through this transition, students are empowered to view themselves as valued members of society, not as second-class academic citizens. This in turn places a responsibility on students to do well and to make a contribution to the public good.

〜

Intrusive intervention offers students—particularly low-performing students or students who face particularly intense challenges (that is to say, *our* students)—the chance to succeed. It does this in large part because it situates these vulnerable students more firmly in the larger culture of the community college. However, intrusive intervention in the form of academic teams is just one of the options utilized by colleges working to enhance student support. In addition, institutions also rely on cohort education as a method for deepening and intensifying student assistance.

I have already explained that teaching community college students is a complicated and difficult task, partly because instructors face what at times is a clear bimodal curve of student abilities. The community college faculty member routinely teaches a classroom of individuals who range in academic abilities from barely literate to highly trained. I remember when I was Dean of Faculty at Middlesex Community College. I taught a class in Human Genetics with nine students. One of my students had a 4th-grade reading level; another had a PhD in bio-linguistics. Despite the small class size, reaching every student in this classroom presented a major challenge. I found myself focusing much of my attention on providing hands-on help to the student with reading difficulties. For the high performing students, and particularly for the PhD student, I merely pointed out additional resources.

These types of unequal adjustments are commonplace in the community college classroom. Teachers of our students have generally had to adapt to an incredibly wide distribution of skill levels. As I explained in the previous chapter, the adaptations have historically manifested in a derivation of traditional pedagogy: to ensure that a critical mass of students grasps subject-matter fundamentals, community college teachers must frequently assume the position of expert and deliver as much information as possible in small, easy-to-understand morsels. The method, we already know, is not particularly effective in our colleges. Fortunately, more successful strategies have begun to take hold. Learning communities, for example, which offer administrators and teachers a way to leverage the extreme variability of student skills to a student's—and to the classroom's—advantage have increased in popularity over the last decade.

Learning communities (Buffington, 2003), also known as communities of practice, emphasize collaborative learning between and among peers. Although they manifest in different ways, a learning community is generally a small group of students who posses varied skill levels. The small group takes a variety of introductory classes together and/or orientation sessions together. Whatever the manifestation, learning communities are used to foster hard skills in the classroom, such as subject fundamentals, and soft skills outside the classroom, such as study habits. Ultimately, learning communities offer underprepared students more individualized attention while allowing proficient students the chance to practice their skills.

We can consider learning communities a different means by which to achieve the same results of academic teams: the communities function as an institutional method through which students create an academic family. For students who attend community colleges, the approach is successful because it is guided by an instructor and provides students with natural, peer-based positive reinforcement. It is also successful because the communities offer the opportunity for supportive familiar interaction through which students can begin to develop (and see reinforced) an academic identity. Additionally, when cohorts of students at a community college are identified by curricular affinity, they develop stronger ties to the college community and may have a better chance of completing than other students.

At Bronx Community College, this dynamic is dramatically exemplified by students in the nursing curriculum. During the clinical experience, nursing students are placed by the college in small cohorts to aid student retention. In respect to retention, the cohorts are very successful. In addition to the dynamic that develops through shared coursework, the cohorts often lead to the formation of less formal study groups. As a result of their close interaction in and outside the clinic, participating students frequently develop informal networks through which they find help navigating other, more personal issues—from babysitting problems and interpersonal relationship issues to academic trouble.

With effective accompanying support services, learning communities can serve many students well. However, traditionalists (and I refer here to both administrators and faculty members) still express suspicion of a model in which students are coached by faculty members and allowed to participate in teaching at a more collaborative level. Administrators and faculty members who prefer the more traditional classroom model, in which a faculty member imparts knowledge while students passively receive information, are often resistant to the concept of learning communities.

Yet, my experience with the efficacy of even informal learning communities is corroborated by research that attests to the effectiveness of the concept and its execution. MDRC, a social policy research organization committed to finding solutions to the intransigent problems facing low-income individuals, researches the effectiveness of many community college pedagogical programs, including the ASAP program. For nearly a decade, Kingsborough Community College of the City University of New York and MDRC studied Kingsborough's learning communities. In 2003, KCC began placing freshmen in peer groups of up to 25 students. The groups took three classes together during their first semester, including one developmental English class. According to MDRC's research, the program increased the average number of credits that students earned and improved students' college experience. Today, KCC is a leader in the learning communities movement.

∼

Learning communities and cohort education can be achieved and intensified through high-impact practices. High-impact practices join curricular and extracurricular concerns through activities that draw on students' time and attention. They require a commitment on the part of the student, but they offer the student closer, more immediate access to peers and to college resources. Learning communities and various manifestations of cohort education are considered high-impact practices, as are service learning opportunities and first-year seminars.

In my experience, high-impact activities can boost student involvement, aid retention, and impact student experiences. Queensborough Community College Academies depend on such activities to effectively reach students. Similar to the academies themselves, the curricular-based activities have been developed by the faculty and take a variety of forms. Some consist of service learning projects, others utilize technology to create electronic-portfolios, others create collaborative assignments, others conduct original research, and others address global and diversity issues. The common denominator for all of these activities is the group-centered structure. Although engaging students in high-impact group-based activities means that instructors may only be able to cover part of the syllabus, when the activities result in impactful learning processes that carry over to other courses, the sacrifice can be worth it.

∽

All of the methods that I've described in this chapter are united by their practical delivery of the culture of care through an *in loco parentis* mandate. Community colleges must provide more than access and more than a passive environment where already-interested or already-engaged students can learn. Community colleges must also meet the needs of those students who have secured access but who are not adept, interested, or engaged in the complexity of postsecondary success. Community college support services must be prepared to provide an appropriate diagnosis of students' needs, must be able to create academic maps that delineate the steps that must be taken to achieve academic, professional, and personal success, and must provide careful monitoring as students progress through their studies. Meanwhile, teachers and support staff must be ready and able to develop and deploy different methodologies to enhance classroom learning. This is what we promise our students. This is the only way we will significantly impact our retention and graduation rates.

In fact, although it may be an unpopular opinion, I would argue that community colleges must go even further. Today's community colleges routinely enroll students who aren't likely to succeed and who therefore fail to produce what has become the expected outcome of either graduation or better employment. However, these outcomes are not necessarily informed by the expectations of community college students. They are instead informed by the expectations of leaders, administrators, and policymakers who are steeped (and often for good, funding-related reasons) in a need for measurable accountability, and who are by and large informed by a postsecondary sector overwhelmingly focused on the baccalaureate degree.

I believe that reaping the rewards of shifting community college academic offerings closer to the guided pathways model proposed and advocated by Bailey, Jaggars, and Jenkins (2015) means redefining student success *away* from the standards imposed by the SRK and *toward* student-led definitions that privilege progression. Our institutions can enroll and engage students in academic teams, restructure student experiences and programs through learning communities, provide ample opportunities for high-impact activities, and generally provide advising and support services that offer obvious and easily graspable opportunities to continue onto pathways toward completion. However, if our institutions don't *also* redefine success through the achievements that our own students recognize as valid, our institutions *and* our students are unlikely to experience meaningful change in any data attesting to achievement.

A better determination of success and achieved outcomes must first take into account the accomplishments and the valid professional experience that many students bring to their community college studies. Former and current members of the military, for example, should be able to secure credit for the on-the-job learning they have acquired. Similarly, students who bring a variety of skills acquired in languages other than English should also be recognized with credit that corresponds to their professional proficiencies.

In addition, those of us associated with community colleges must recognize that for many students, *progression* and *acquisition* may be as or more important than *completion*. Not all community college students are recent high school graduates who seek postsecondary graduation. In fact, it is widely recognized that community college enrollment soars during economic downturns. Many of our students attend community college to wait out an economic slough, or turn to community colleges to acquire relevant skills in their industry, or simply seek the skills that will allow them to change careers. Companies also approach community colleges with contract-based proposals through which to train individuals in needed skills. While our institutions must offer a navigable pathway to postsecondary completion and graduation, we must also meet the needs of the many students interested in progression and acquisition. This is another way community college leaders, administrators, faculty members, support staff, and policymakers can put student need first. By providing individualized programs of study, our institutions can help facilitate the broadest possible range of student success.

Chapter 5

Funding the Change

Revising institutional missions, shifting models of pedagogy, better integrating remediation and developmental education, and initiating meaningful student support services will undoubtedly be costly. Community colleges cannot adopt real widespread structural or systemic change without significant and stable financial backing. Our institutions have to be economically sustainable to implement the far more comprehensive—yet squarely student-centered—focus I advocate. Simply put, without more, and more permanent resources, we cannot make good on our institutional promise. Our schools can provide lasting and navigable paths to achievement for *all* the students who access the education we offer *only* when financial viability is both certain and permanent.

Achieving fiscal viability is not a challenge that community colleges can meet alone. Although the institutions receive federal, state, and local support, the money has never been enough, and it is most certainly not enough now. Case in point: despite the fact that community colleges are responsible for educating nearly 50 percent of today's undergraduates, the institutions historically receive about 27 percent of the total federal, state, and local revenue designated for public postsecondary schools (Mullin, 2010). If we want to enact widespread change, community college leaders, presidents, and boards of trustees must identify and develop strategies for building diverse and continuous financial resources.

We already know that funding is influenced by public perception. Accordingly, the first step of a sound development strategy depends on educating our communities and our community leaders about the economic value offered by our schools and our students. Too often, the public perceives that a postsecondary education, even at a community college, is for individual gain rather than the public good. In addition, a community's older taxpayers who attended more selective colleges may have a hard time understanding why money must be spent on individuals who did not do well in high school. Fiscally conservative taxpayers may view a community college as a kind of charity, a "last gas station before the desert," where individuals who don't deserve to be in school get the education that others worked hard to attain.

These of course are the community members that our leaders, presidents, and trustees most need to educate. They—and the public at large—must be made aware of the comprehensive economic value of a well-educated and well-trained local workforce. We can aid this awareness by pointing out the tangible fiscal benefits of taxpayer investment in our institutions. It is relatively simple to demonstrate the positive impact on the overall tax base provided by a greater number of community college graduates. When community college graduates procure good jobs, they pay greater income taxes and are able to purchase new houses and pay higher property taxes. Community members who understand this relationship are far more likely to perceive student-centered community college initiatives like the ones I've described in this book as crucial to the community's economy and *not* as uncontrolled expenditures.

Public perception is crucial to community college viability because public perception translates to political perception, and political perception translates to per-capita funding. Consequently, community college leaders, presidents, and trustees must engage in widespread campaigning to communicate institutional value. According to the Center on Budget and Policy Priorities, New York state's higher education per-capita funding was lower in 2015 than it was in 2008. The decrease in dollars tells us that we have not yet mounted a convincing argument. Effective campaigns should be modeled after the campaigns conducted by colleges that depend on millage rates to fund the construction of new facilities. They should include information that will communicate both the college's value and the immediate and long-term economic impact of proposals designed to increase retention, completion, and graduation rates.

Because campaigning for community colleges can mean waging an uphill battle, any convincing campaign will also require the cultivation of strong alliances with local elected officials. Rather than entering into informal or otherwise distant relationships, however, officials and policymakers must be made *allies* in the task of community college transformation. This seemingly simple task is often difficult because institutions that depend solely on the goodwill of elected representatives are already under a great deal of pressure to maintain or reduce operating budgets. To surmount this difficulty, community college leaders must reach and partner with powerful agents of change. Champions must be identified and asked for support. To continue generating goodwill, the campaign must persist in efforts to keep the public at large aware of—and convinced by—institutional initiatives.

Today is the day for building an effective campaign. President Obama's proposal for a tuition-free two years speaks to the community college's national import. His call to arms, combined with the goal to increase the number of community college graduates by 5 million in the year 2020, amounts to a national agenda that echoes much of what I've argued in this book. The national spotlight now trained on our colleges offers an opportunity to gain community and political support for funding that will transform our schools into the student-centered institutions that will enact our missions and our promise. It is up to us, as community college leaders and supporters, to translate this national agenda into a local imperative.

If the perception of community colleges has been mixed in recent decades, the perception of community college funding has been decidedly negative. This reflects the difficulty of landing on viable and popular (or at least *not unpopular*) strategies for funding an institution that has always been asked to open its doors to everyone and proficiently educate everyone. The per-capita funding mechanism on which community colleges depend is necessary and can be used to the colleges' advantage, but it is currently unstable and inefficient. Over time, it has made our institutions too dependent on new student enrollments: as students graduate or more often drop out, a new crop of recent graduates *must* replace them so that the average headcount, and therefore the average pool of resources, remains roughly the same.

It is no secret that this funding mechanism has led to a fiscal focus trained on new enrollees rather than on current students. For most community colleges, the stakes are just too high. The threat of losing major resources to the ebbs and flows of the student population is too formidable. This was not always the case, of course. When the schools were small and the system disorganized, community colleges did not draw enough public resources to merit meaningful pushback. However, now that community colleges have expanded to accommodate ever growing student populations, operational costs have ballooned. The dramatic popularity of our schools means that our institutions have consistently been in need of more resources to meet ever wider, deeper, and more disparate student needs. To ensure the continuation of open-access policies that have been valued by many communities and by the federal government, the colleges turned with vigor to local and state sources.

In those earlier days, fiscal support through local taxation generally supplied the most logical and strongest foundation because early community colleges were more closely aligned with secondary schools. Local taxation provided the majority of money on a per-student basis, and states provided smaller funds to offset divisive district variability. Over time, the colleges necessitated an ever larger outlay of local and state funds to ensure the low-cost tuitions promised by their open-access policies (Cohen, Brawer, & Kisker, 2013) and to also facilitate continued coverage of increased operational costs.

As the expanding colleges have made more demands on communities, local-level support has leveled off and is now in its decline. The case of California stands as a dramatic example. Up to the 1970s, California's community college system was one of the most comprehensive in the nation. The system drew much of its fiscal strength from levies that promised its community colleges a percentage of property taxes as set by local school boards. The mechanism, while it conferred necessary stability, was far from perfect. Districts, even closely neighboring districts, saw radical differences in the resources available for students because taxes were not uniformly assessed and because school boards did not share the same needs (Picus, 1991). Measures to equalize funding through redistributed taxes were a largely unpopular (and ultimately temporary) solution.

California taxpayers constantly chafed against mandatory levies supporting what appeared to be an unceasing rise in operational costs for postsecondary schooling (Picus, 1991). When Proposition 13 passed in 1978 as a more permanent solution to the community-college problem, it passed with enthusiastic voter support (Picus, 1991). The proposition did not ensure equitable funding between institutions, but it did ensure that property taxes could only be collected on the basis of 1 percent of assessed property value and that assessed value could only rise 2 percent a year.

In the short run, Proposition 13 was a boon to home-owning taxpayers. But in the long run, it marked, however obliquely, the end of an era of what was even then only somewhat stable funding for community colleges. Immediately after the proposition passed, the state of California was on the hook to make up the funding that local communities would no longer cover.

In partial if perhaps only implicit response to Proposition 13, funding for community colleges across the nation began to shift. In most cases, the responsibility for the majority of community college financing began to transfer from local to state governments. This happened despite the fact that the zeitgeist at the time favored open-access policies that were federally endorsed and unevenly but still institutionally enacted. By the early 1980s, community colleges in California represented a rather comprehensive future for these schools in which open-access policies were systematically (although usually indirectly) rolled back via a reliance on state appropriations and a correspondent reliance on higher tuitions (Cohen, Brawer, & Kisker, 2013).

Increasing tuition has always posed an obvious problem for community college students and for community colleges' open-access, democratic-minded priorities. But occasionally higher tuitions have also always had to provide a necessary, if still only partial, solution. Higher tuitions can sometimes be imperative because the transfer from local to state funding means that institutional financial security will continue to be elusive into the indeterminate future. State budgets simply cannot guarantee community colleges the sort of stable, long-term funding to aid comprehensive or even predictable development.

In fact, for most states, funding for all forms of higher education is one of the largest discretionary line items in the state budget. Although in general, the higher education sector is a high priority, it usually falls a little too far down the list of items requiring substantial state outlay. This means that the money available for higher education usually depends on what is left over after items deemed more important have been subsidized. Line items in the "more important" category often include necessities that are just as important to a community, including Medicaid, K–12 education, general infrastructure costs, and prisons (Katsinas & Tollefson, 2009).

Back in California, the problems associated with funding an institution according to a state discretionary budget have long been on display. Following the passage of Proposition 13, unpredictability has become an ironically permanent feature of the state's community college system. That unpredictability has never really improved. In fact, according to the Public Policy Institute of California (2013), the contemporary financial picture of California's community colleges reflects the perpetuation of insecurity. Researchers Bohn, Reyes, and Johnson (2013) write that in California, "the most common feature in the long-term budget picture for the community college system has been the year to year volatility in the level of funding" (p. 2).

∾

When it comes to appropriations, community colleges have mostly (although not always) followed in California's footsteps. As indicated above, communities and community members do not always intuitively grasp the import of community colleges, and community colleges do not always make a persuasive case for their import. Consequently, most community colleges look to *both* local and state sources for funding. They also, and often even increasingly, look to more meaningful federal sources for support. Obama's call for a tuition-free two years of community college comes at a time when some community college leaders and administrators have found it necessary to increase tuition rates to the point that many low-income families have a difficult time meeting the financial requirement. It therefore brings with it the hope for a substantial influx of federal resources.

Even when considered cumulatively, current local, federal, and tuition-based resources do not equate to permanent stability. As leaders, administrators, faculty members, and policymakers, we well know that while extant sources of funding are absolutely crucial, they do not enable our schools to consistently avoid the pitfalls of unpredictable state budgets. In the best of times, our colleges must constantly strategize and plan to make the most of budgetary windfalls (no matter how relative or temporary) and inconsistently surging enrollments. In the worst of times, our colleges must accommodate significant cutbacks and determine and execute the least disruptive ways to trim costs.

$\sim$

Today, we have just emerged from some of the worst of times. Starting in late 2007 and extending through 2009, during what we now know as the Great Recession, community colleges saw significant enrollment spikes *and* significant budgetary cutbacks. Enrollment spikes are usually welcome, but the aftereffects our institutions began to feel as soon as the Great Recession drew to a close indicated that the spikes that accompanied this recession were more problematic than promising.

The individual numbers vary widely, of course, but according to AACC's Senior Vice President of Government Relations and Research, David Baime, average national enrollment for community colleges generally jumped nearly 25 percent from the 2007–2008 to the 2010–2011 academic years (as quoted in Tyson, 2014). The leap was attributed in large part to the difficult financial times experienced by many Americans. As we know from rich historical experience, recessions usually drive jobseekers to community colleges in search of acquiring new, more relevant job skills.

The enrollment spike at community colleges was also ascribed to the impact of the Great Recession on so many *other* postsecondary institutions. By 2008, most institutions were hit, and hit hard, by state budget cuts. In response, many schools had to transfer some more of the budgetary burden onto students' shoulders. Across the board, many schools increased tuitions to make up shortfalls. Even though the hikes at many institutions were relatively small, they still impacted students. For instance, tuitions at public 4-year postsecondary schools only rose by an average of .1 percent from 2008–2009 to 2009–2010 (Zumeta, 2011), but the figure proved too high for many families, and students increasingly opted out.

While student enrollments at 4-year universities remained flat or fell during the Great Recession, student enrollments at community colleges rose, and rose sharply. This was the case despite a relatively higher increase in tuition rates at the community colleges—2.6 percent on average (Zumeta, 2011). Ultimately, the students for whom community colleges had always been attractive attended college despite the tuition hikes (and despite the fact that those hikes were even more difficult for them to absorb). These students and the many others who might have matriculated to more traditional 4-year schools but who instead sought relative refuge in our schools ensured that the institutions remained in a strong position on the postsecondary field.

During the Great Recession, students entered community colleges for the same reasons that students have always come to our institutions. The colleges offer the benefit of proximity and enable students to remain local and therefore keep general educational costs, such as those associated with living and commuting, low. The colleges also offer the benefit of a still comparatively low tuition. For many community college students, the tuition was made even lower by the major Great Recession-era expansion of the Pell Grant program. Many students, particularly students who may not have been otherwise able to meet higher rates of tuition, took advantage of the 43 percent rise in the average Pell Grant and the 80 percent rise in number of grant recipients that occurred between 2006–2007 and 2010–2011 (Johnson, 2014).

~

Although community colleges remained vital during the Great Recession, in a reverberation of the historical challenges related to economic stability, the vitality was not—and is still not—stable. Most leaders and administrators at community colleges know that the largess that accrues through contextual increases in enrollment is only ever temporary. While the jobseekers who enter community colleges in times of economic hardship *can* help increase college coffers, they generally do so for only a finite period of time. Their participation in the colleges cannot be counted on beyond the life of the financial downturn because when the economy begins to rebound, jobseekers often return to the market, seeking, and more often finding, jobs.

In addition, economic slowdowns and recessions hit both members of the public and public institutions alike, and both are slow to recover. Consequently, the Great Recession wreaked havoc on community colleges' already unpredictable, volatile funding structures. This is the reason why some tuitions rose in the first place. Local and state treasuries and budgets were hit incredibly hard by the economic downturn, and the pressing needs surrounding the implementation of Medicaid, K–12 education, infrastructure development, prisons, and other higher priority items pushed appropriations for higher education even further down the list of budgetary expenditures.

In states that were hit hardest by the recession, the influx of students combined with lower appropriations resulted in cuts to per-student funding that remained more-or-less permanent. These are the kinds of cuts that an increase in community college tuition tries to but cannot totally repair. Per-student funding cuts do not often force the same kinds of decisions as required by absolute cuts, but community colleges leaders, administrators, and faculty members still must scramble to serve far more students with far fewer resources (Johnson, 2014).

Currently, the nation is experiencing a growing economy (Miller & Chandra, 2015). Community college campuses have consequently experienced lower enrollment levels as students have begun testing market conditions for jobs. Although fiscally responsible community college leaders and administrators may have accumulated some reserves during times of increased enrollments to offset the effects of inevitable economic variability, only so much can be offset. Further, state recuperation lags behind the economy, and tax coffers require a longer cycle than that of businesses to replenish losses. This is how America's economic turnaround becomes ironically problematic for community college operations.

$\sim$

Ultimately, the Great Recession simply accelerated what was by 2007 an already clear path toward state disinvestment in community colleges. The California community college system signaled the possibility way back in the 1970s. But the tendency toward disinvestment had become a certain trend by the first years of the twenty-first century. In fact, between 2000 and 2010, state appropriations for community colleges had already fallen 20 percent (Kirshstein & Hurlbert, 2012); the Great Recession merely contributed to an extant exodus.

As local and state sources have markedly turned away from reinstating even a hint of former funding levels, community college leaders now reckon with the inevitable permanence of what had always been a longstanding reality. Any associated surprise among leaders or administrators is only due to the fact that the recession-related cuts were so much more dramatic than what had preceded them. Before, during, and after the Great Recession, community college leaders, administrators, and policymakers remained committed to providing wide access to postsecondary education at low costs. The acute budgetary issues simply meant that we, as postsecondary school leaders and administrators, had to take an even closer and more serious look at the resources that could be used to disengage institutional reliance on state support and other appropriations.

I believe that in this post-recession era, when our institutions might be suffering but our mission is nationally recognized as more relevant than ever, we face a critical moment for community college funding. Leaders, administrators, and trustees must work now to uncover and develop more permanent and more stable sources of funding. We cannot effectuate the very real reform required by our institutions by simply rearranging expenditure plans. It is now, alongside a federal cry for affordability and a communal cry for achievement, that we must explore every avenue open to ensuring our institutional sustainability.

～

To enact the change necessary for our schools to operate as student-centered institutions devoted to both access and achievement, we must secure broad financial viability through proactive revenue diversification. This means that community college leaders, administrators, and trustees must look beyond state contributions. We must look first to expanded federal funding, including federal grants and contracts, then to strong and strategic business alliances, then to traditional fundraising efforts, and finally to philanthropic and private foundation initiatives and awards for our funds. We must also consider how best to ensure that our institutions run smartly and efficiently without sacrificing the quality education we work to provide.

First, the federal government's contribution is one of our most crucial revenue streams, and we must turn to its availability with vigor. This, of course, has not always been the case. Despite the government's early and vociferously stated interest in promoting a widely educated population, it generally maintained a blurry focus on the funding required for effective postsecondary schooling. After World War II, the federal government extended meaningful grants and other funding measures to universities engaged in approved research, but these same coffers were not opened to community colleges.

In fact, federal funding to community colleges (and most postsecondary schools) has remained indirect. Both the G.I. Bill and the first Higher Education Act of 1965, two of the first widespread instances of federal funding for postsecondary education, infused less selective institutions in general, and community colleges in particular, with federal money. Because community colleges absorbed mostly underprepared but still-deserving students, the pressure on selective colleges to accept veterans was diminished, and the more traditional 4-year institutions were able to benefit as well.

Today, federal funding is still indirect, but it is much more comprehensive. The indirect federal funding that arrives at postsecondary institutions like community colleges via federal student aid, such as Pell Grants, work-study grants, and supplemental education opportunity grants, makes up nearly 99 percent of the U.S. Department of Education's contemporary outlay (Mullin, 2010). In this manner, the federal government indirectly funds the postsecondary aspirations of millions of students. In the 2013–2014 academic year, 3.5 million of the 10.5 million students who attended community college received Pell Grants. The support resulted in 11 billion dollars of federal money directed to offset the costs associated with community college attendance (AACC, 2015).

In addition to its comprehensive programs for students, the federal government also provides indirect funding via federal grants and contracts. These funds, usually extended on a one-time basis, are available to all postsecondary schools for the purposes of research, training, or similar activities. Over the last thirty years, the federal funds available for these types of grants and contracts have grown by 10 to 20 percent and have contributed in substantive ways to offset state funding drawdowns (Keener, 2002; Phelan, 2014).

Community colleges generally receive grants awarded by the Trade Adjustment Assistance Community College and Career Training (better known by the unbelievably cumbersome acronym TAACCCT). Since 2011, TAACCCT has awarded nearly 1.5 billion dollars in grants to colleges (Perez, 2014). Like so many other avenues of funding, the money extended by government programs like TAACCCT offers a necessary, albeit complicated, windfall.

The money has undeniably helped community colleges develop initiatives and programs. For example, the Community College of Denver used its TAACCCT money to develop initiatives to accelerate developmental education and build programs to meet industry needs through the Colorado Online Training Consortium. At Kingsborough Community College of the City University of New York, TAACCCT funds enabled the establishment of stackable credentials for medical billers, medical assistants, EMTs, and community health workers.

Yet, the money also poses some significant problems for community colleges. The grants and contracts provide practical injections of cash into institutions and institutional programs, but the funds offered by the grants and contracts are only temporary investments. No matter how substantive a role the awards play, the resources they offer cannot offer a permanent substitute for more stable, and more efficient, funding.

Whether or not the funds provide a measure of stability, community college leaders, administrators, and trustees must utilize all existent, if also indirect and temporary, opportunities for federal funding. Additionally, we must campaign for the federal funds that will be necessary to enact America's College Promise outlined by President Obama. According to Obama's plan, the federal outlay for the initiative will be about 60 billion dollars. Because the initiative broadens access to our institutions and asks our institutions to augment transfer and occupational programs and integrate evidence-based research into enhancing student outcomes, it may provide a substantive path by which to enact the changes for which I argue.

~

Of course, at the same time that community colleges advocate for the money necessary to achieve the federal vision, leaders and administrators must also carefully investigate the expectations attached to government funding, particularly funding in the form of grants and contracts. The expectations are complicated because they both help and hinder our colleges. On the one hand, federal grants and contracts provide community colleges the funds and direction for development. On the other hand, the expectations can impede community colleges by significantly narrowing the direction in which a college can develop.

Expectations are usually informed by the money's specific purpose. The colleges receive federal grants and contracts to enact particular initiatives or to develop particular programs. While the awards and grants are welcome, they can't help but contribute toward uneven institutional development. They sometimes even work as an obstacle within the wider system of community colleges. For example, when a college implements a training program required by a particular federal grant, it may have to divert previous institutional and/or financial focus away from programs with credit-bearing courses to programs without credit-bearing courses. Sometimes the diversion dovetails with institutional priorities, but sometimes it does not.

I've seen this situation play out firsthand at Bronx Community College. The college is actively engaged in CUNY 2020, a program that provides funding for the expansion of the only AutoTech program at a public college in NYC. The college is also very much involved in promoting its Institute for Sustainable Energy and its Geospatial Center. These programs are incredibly important to the local economy and have been aided in their development by federal funding. There will be a time, however, and probably in the not too distant future, when competition for space and resources will restrict further development in this direction.

In addition to uneven development *within* an institution, Phelan reports (2014), and I myself have seen, that the competitive nature of government grants and contracts encourages divisions *between* institutions. As I've continuously argued, the community college sector is already incredibly variable. The competition for funding in which all schools must enter often widens divisions that already separate the schools. A major point of contention in this regard is the observed phenomenon that money begets money.

Large community colleges that are relatively flush already have more resources and can therefore command more resources. In fact, these larger, richer institutions frequently employ grant writers and are therefore well positioned to attract the funds necessary for institutional development.

Community colleges that are smaller, less resource rich, and often rural cannot compete on the same scale. Although these descriptors apply to the colleges that happen to constitute the majority of the American community college sector, these institutions are only rarely moneyed (ruralalliance.org). These schools usually do not have the same resources as larger colleges and usually cannot employ staff members such as grant writers. Consequently, these colleges simply cannot take the same advantage of the government's competitive opportunities. In this way, competitive funding can contribute to retrenching the very divisions that many leaders and administrators in the community college sector have spent years working to overcome.

The necessity to compete for *any* available funding can split institutional focus and exacerbate the existing challenges posed by too-diffuse efforts to be everything to every potential student. It can also widen the gaps between our schools. Accordingly, when working to diversify funding streams, community college leaders, administrators, and trustees must take advantage of but also must *avoid* placing too high a value on government grants and contracts. This will help ensure that an already too-general mission (for example) is not made even more difficult to enact and execute.

≈

When it comes to revenue diversification, opportunities for contractual alliances with community businesses should be considered as important to community college development as government funding. Accordingly, after community college administrators and leaders look to competitive federal sources for revenue diversification, they then must turn toward more actively courting the strategic business and community relationships that can lead to substantive contracts and other remunerative programs for community college students.

The intentional development of strategic alliances with local businesses is in some ways a contemporary expansion of the contract programs that started leaving a mark on community colleges in the 1980s. Of course, just like those programs, the potential revenue streams posed by business and community alliances are complicated. Namely, the programs built to support the alliances often rely on the same sort of competitive funding offered by federal grants and awards. The programs can therefore encourage a diverted focus—this time along company lines—that makes comprehensive development so difficult for community colleges.

The efforts among community college leaders and administrators to develop strong business alliances can also be controversial because of the issue of reimbursement. The relationships frequently work through a payback structure whereby the cost of educating participants is reimbursed in accordance with a strict, performance-based timeline. The payoff for students and for institutions can be considerable, but unless student-specific requirements are met—such as completed training and job placement at a specified salary within a specified period of time—payment can also be elusive (Mellow & Heelan, 2008).

Accordingly, and not at all unlike the reception of those early contract training efforts, the popularity of the current programs is mixed. The programs can be construed as a drain on resources: they generally emphasize noncredit-bearing courses and often provide a return on investment only when certain, highly specific criteria, are met. However, the programs can also lay valuable inroads into communities and businesses and can contribute to the significant likelihood of turning noncredit participants into degree-pursuing students (Mellow & Heelan, 2008). In addition, it likely goes without saying that these programs can also help forge the connections between colleges and communities that are so necessary and valuable.

I have been lucky in my career to see the benefits of these types of alliances. In fact, one of the best professional experiences of my career was at Corning Community College. Corning Community College is a regional college, which means that we did not have a particular county legislature to approve our budget. The board of trustees was the official employer of the college, and we were, at the time, the only institution of education in New York state—elementary, secondary, or tertiary—that was not unionized. This incredible degree of autonomy was counterweighted by the responsibility to meet payroll. Every August we borrowed money from a local bank to have enough cash flow to meet the September payroll; then, we hoped that our predictions were on target and the student enrollments met our budget requirements.

Corning Incorporated was a major supporter of the college. When the company began shifting its focus from glass manufacturing to fiber optics manufacturing, it also began talking about building a plant in Pennsylvania. Corning Inc. considered the Pennsylvania labor force better trained and better suited for manufacturing the fiber. Leaders and administrators at CCC did not want Corning Inc. to leave. We therefore offered a proposal for facilitating the conversion of a portion of the existing workforce from glass making and blowing to fiber technology. Happily, the Corning Inc. executives wanted to keep work in the county of Steuben. They were skeptical, however, that CCC could deliver the terms of the proposal.

Speed was of the essence. At CCC, we created an 18-month part-time curriculum that could train existing workers as fiber optic technicians through coursework completed on Thursday evenings, Fridays, and Saturdays. The company released its workers on Friday, and the workers donated their time on Saturdays. The company paid the tuition for the workers and provided *in situ* facilities. At the end of the contract, CCC kept the equipment. Although the proposals' terms were rigorous, the program was a resounding success. The regional college governance structure, the goodwill and confidence that Corning Inc. had for CCC, and the cooperation of the workers and their union contributed to a most successful contract arrangement. In fact, the curriculum is still offered by CCC.

To engage in similarly successful programs, community colleges' leaders and administrators have to ask whether their institutions can accommodate the needs of local employers without unfairly disrupting the mission of the institution. This is often a very difficult question to answer, partly because economic viability is such a pressing matter for so many college leaders and administrators, and partly because community college funders are not disinterested citizens. In the above case, it worked beautifully, and in most cases, it does. Of course, sometimes the relationship does not work, and if that happens, it is important that both the institution's mission and the relationships the institution has developed with the businesses remain strong.

~

Like government funds, strategic business alliances that lead to meaningful college development are crucial for community colleges. However, in addition to securing government funding and community and business relationships, leaders and administrators of community colleges must also look to the models for developing prosperous endowments and foundations long used by 4-year public and private institutions. It may not be in our best interest to reproduce the educational model provided by more traditional 4-year postsecondary schools, but it is imperative that we follow their lead in fundraising efforts.

Recent attempts to build such models at community colleges amount to a new recognition that engaging in far more comprehensive fundraising campaigns is an absolute necessity for institutional viability. Effective fundraising is much more than a way to increase the college's financial resources: it is an important component of a college's position in its community. It is also a means by which community members can validate the community college's institutional import and communicate it more widely. In an abstract sense, the validation shows students the import of their work. In a practical sense, the validation can influence elected officials when the time comes to fund college operations. When the pillars of a community buy into their community college, they potentially influence the employers in a position to offer jobs to the graduates of that college.

Community college fundraising efforts have recently begun to flourish, but they must be made a major component of colleges' funding programs. Like the other revenue streams I've discussed, scaling up is not necessarily straightforward. In the case of traditional fundraising, the colleges only began to purposefully implement development programs for fundraising efforts in the early 1990s. And even then they were "late to the game," according to Walter Dillingham Jr. (as quoted in Marcus, 2013). The institutions' late arrival explains why in 2011 community colleges received only about 1 million dollars per institution in voluntary donations. Meanwhile, the average research university received 90 million dollars (Kaplan, 2013).

Scaling up is challenging for community colleges for many reasons. For one, our schools, unlike more traditional 4-year institutions, have not always worked to foster a culture of giving back. Our institutions did not always perceive a pressing need for funding beyond that provided by local and state sources. Whereas most established baccalaureate-granting colleges have historically relied heavily on alumni to establish annual funds and capital campaigns, our institutions have not. Additionally, our alumni base is often perceived as too small and their giving capacity too little, to contribute much to fundraising efforts.

Today, most community college leaders and administrators recognize that despite any historical and alumni-related hurdles, traditional fundraising efforts represent a crucial contemporary means for securing more stable resources. Many leaders and administrators also understand that fundraising is no longer restricted to alumni-specific pools, nor does it necessary require throwing expensive galas or wooing donors with traditional displays of extravagance (although such efforts do have their place). Rather, fundraising for community colleges functions much like fundraising for community organizations: it depends on friends, foundations, the generosity of community leaders, and the work ethic of persistent fundraisers to raise money.

More often than not, fundraising means—and in fact, absolutely depends on—establishing and fostering relationships with alumni and community members that extend far beyond institutional walls. Again, and as ever, the case has to be made that the college is essential to and for the community. This could be because of the workforce development that takes place at the college (in this case, relationships can act as an avenue to corporate gifts), or because of the artistic benefits offered by the college, or because of the benefits of the physical facilities offered by the college for communal use. Further, although galas, golf outings, and events of this sort are not effective fundraisers, they are exceptionally good *friendraisers*. And for community colleges, raising friends is an imperative.

In fact, to implement fundraising on a more comprehensive scale, community colleges must develop close connections and meaningful relationships with influential community members. This is often done through the kind of campaigning I refer to above in which all participants in a community are made aware of and are helped to understand and appreciate a college's academic and social mission. Community members will not validate the work done by a community college with their donations unless the case has been made clearly and explicitly that the college meaningfully contributes to the welfare of the community at large.

The community colleges with the most successful fundraising efforts devote separate departments to fundraising work and tap the expertise of professionals to ensure that the college gathers a return on its investment. The most successful community colleges also recognize that fundraising efforts pay off in truly practical ways through funding college endowments. In my experience, campaigns to create endowments are the most difficult for community colleges to mount. Often, community college donors identify with programs or with particular groups of students. Perhaps their experience with the college reflects the institution's too-diffuse identity (informed, perhaps, by a cafeteria-style model of education or by a weak, unachievable mission). An endowment may therefore feel too abstract. But while it may be challenging to fund, endowments are crucial for institutional stability. Indeed, endowments can help protect institutions from external, contextual financial vicissitudes, such as those caused by fluctuations in enrollments and economic downturns (and upswings).

An incredibly successful fundraising effort at Queenborough Community College offers an instructive story. However unlikely, the effort began with my introduction to the campus, when I first became acquainted with the Holocaust Resource Center. During my tour, I found the center in a dark, windowless room in the basement of a library. Despite the fact that Queens County has the largest number of Holocaust survivors after Israel, this important facility was tucked away, as if it were a matter of shame and neglect. Perhaps its status as an afterthought reflected the college's contemporary student population: it is no longer Jewish and is roughly equally divided among Whites, Blacks, Hispanics, and Asians.

Later, when considering campus efforts that might benefit from fundraising, I remembered this seemingly forgotten center, housed in our library's basement. I understood that the Holocaust was caused by what many consider to be the ultimate expression of prejudice. I also realized that the great majority of students at Queensborough had been the subjects of prejudice (and in some cases were still the subjects of prejudice) at some point in their lives. I therefore embarked upon a quest to bring the Holocaust Resource Center from the basement of the library to the forefront of our college, where it could stand as a reminder of and a call for equality.

Although the fundraising effort started small, it soon grew into a relationship between private businesses, community members, and the public sector. Through rigorous community outreach, our efforts raised 5.6 million dollars from the public sector to build a new Holocaust Resource Center at the entrance of the college. We also raised 2.3 million dollars from private funders to ensure that programming for the center will continue in perpetuity. Even the federal government realized the worthiness of our cause: we received a matching grant from the National Endowment for the Humanities.

The Holocaust Resource Center is now a beacon of civility in Queens and a boon to the mission of our college. A decidedly multicultural board that represents all of the nationalities that populate the Queens community advises the center. It has been recognized as a Hate Crimes Resource Center for the City of New York and is present at all community events that deal with hate crimes. Our Holocaust Resource Center is dedicated to the proposition that prejudice negatively affects all of us, and it directly informs (and is informed by) college research and pedagogy. Today, student interns work with Holocaust survivors to learn about the impact of prejudice and integrate their findings into coursework and community service.

~

My experience at Queensborough shows what can be done when a college yokes together a wide variety of resources to meet its goals. There is, however, at least one more piece of the funding puzzle. Helping to bridge the funding gap between government funds and grants, business alliances, and fundraising efforts is the rise of reform-related funding increasingly available to community colleges through private organizations and foundations. Such organizations frequently operate via the same competitive funding models as government grants and contracts and business-based contract-training programs. However, organizations such as the Kellogg Foundation, the Bill and Melinda Gates Foundation, the Alfred P. Sloan Foundation, and the Lumina Foundation do not pit colleges against one another in a race for limited funding. Instead, they aim to provide funds for scaled-up approaches to fostering community colleges' holistic health.

The Alfred P. Sloan Foundation, for example, has been instrumental in the comprehensive development of community colleges through the Community College Research Center that the foundation helped to found. As implicitly noted throughout this work, the Community College Research Center at Columbia's Teachers College is a pre-eminent organization that conducts credible research on community colleges. I have been fortunate enough to have served as a member of its Advisory Board. With the help of the Alfred P. Sloan Foundation, the board has been able to maintain objective research that acts not as an advocate for community colleges, but as an academic mirror to reflect the effectiveness or lack thereof in community college education. The result has been rigorous research that aids community college development. Through careful management, the original funding for CCRC from the Alfred P. Sloan Foundation now exceeds 20 million dollars. Of course, more is needed to continue conducting top-notch research, but we have in this organization a way to eliminate unhelpful rhetoric about our institutions and to use established research methodologies to make our case.

The Bill and Melinda Gates Foundation also provides crucial contributions to community college improvement by making funds available to colleges for important work. To realize its goals to make community colleges key to widespread postsecondary success, for example, the foundation implemented Completion by Design, and it will soon implement the Pathways Project. The former offers competitive grants to institutions to first promote the identification of achievement-related data. The funds also help to develop and apply new data-driven measures to enable the transformation of the community college experience for low-income students under 26. The latter, the Pathways Project, will launch in partnership with the AACC. It promises to promote developmental capacity for the sort of guided pathways approach advocated by Bailey, Jaggars, and Jenkins (2015).

While the Alfred P. Sloan Foundation and the Bill and Melinda Gates Foundation are crucial to the future success of our schools, in the world of philanthropic efforts, the Lumina Foundation likely claims the highest profile initiatives. Achieving the Dream, which began in community colleges in 2003, is its broad attempt to identify evidence-based intervention strategies. The application of these strategies targets low-income students and students of color and focuses on pulling up their school performance and aiding their ability to better reach higher rates of retention and graduation. Scaling up successful implementation continues to remain Achieving the Dream's major goal.

One of the more surprising benefits of the Achieving the Dream program has been its focus on educating and training administrators. As in many postsecondary institutions, administrators at community colleges often achieve their positions by rising through the ranks. Only a few programs, such as Florida State, ACE Community Colleges, and the Association of Community College Trustees, provide intensive training for aspiring administrators. Community colleges are extremely complex institutions, and the Achieving the Dream project goes a long way to provide coaching for existing administrators and to enhance the accountability and effectiveness of the college. Now that Achieving the Dream is a self-sustaining program and now that colleges have to contribute to participate, it has become a de-facto form of institutional training that will continue to yield results as more colleges enter the program.

The strategies integrated into community colleges by the funds available through initiatives like Achieving the Dream *can* promote the same sort of diverted focus problems as those inadvertently fostered by other forms of competitive funding. But they often don't. The reason is that initiatives advocated by private foundations and organizations are far more likely to be comprehensively reform-minded. They therefore focus on systemic issues related to retention and graduation that affect many (if not most) community colleges. Further, funding from foundations and organizations intent on reform are usually squarely focused on identification, implementation, and scalability. The broad applicability can go a long way toward promoting unification rather than division among the community colleges in the postsecondary field.

∽

Over the last few years, community colleges have come a long way toward effectively diversifying funding streams. But there is no denying the fact that the institutions continue to occupy an incredibly difficult financial position. Further, when it comes to the outcomes of the various means by which community colleges have attempted to identify and tap into different funding streams, it is not always easy to gauge success. Are the time-consuming, far-reaching efforts of community colleges well spent? Do they lead to better, higher quality outcomes for our students? Can we say from our vantage point in 2016 that community colleges have come a good ways toward securing the kind of diverse funding that will ensure institutional sustainability in the coming years? Although the short answer has to be no, the long answer leaves at least a little room for yes. Fundraising and the funding available from private foundations are helping our institutions to mature into a more cohesive, more stable system.

～

Of course, while community colleges continue to explore ways to enhance revenue, the economic and political climate means that our institutions must also continue figuring out how to do more with substantially less. This means that leaders and administrators cannot only look outside our institutions for resources. We must also take a focused look *inside* the walls of our institutions to determine and execute the usually complicated and controversial measures by which efficiency can be ensured. To better adapt to contemporary fiscal and enrollment-related challenges, we must make difficult decisions about how to best run our institutions.

This still means taking a hard look at tuition. Many years ago, when it first became clear that the traditional funding sources were tapering off, we had to consider how far and how much to sacrifice the low tuitions through which our colleges embodied an open-access and democratically energized education. Now that the stability of traditional funding sources has all but disappeared, we must continue to consider the question implicitly posed by tuition. Can we keep tuitions low? How low?

Fortunately, many leaders and administrators (myself included), and many policymakers, want to answer *yes* and *as low as possible*. The Obama administration has made this a clear priority for the federal government, and community college visionaries like those in Tennessee and Oregon are working ahead of the Obama administration to supply a tuition-free community college education to their students.

But we must also be honest with ourselves: tuition-free education is simply not yet a reality. At most community colleges, tuitions, which despite recent rises are still relatively low (especially in comparison to 4-year schools), are unfortunately just not low *enough*. This is illustrated by my own institution, which, as I mentioned in Chapter 1, worked in the fall of 2015 to close the financial gap between 1,584 students and their completion of an associate's degree. As I reported, we were able to meet the needs of most of the students. We were not able to meet the needs of all of them.

Bronx Community College is certainly not an anomaly. On average, community colleges charged tuition of nearly $3,300 during the 2013–2014 academic year (Baum & Ma, 2013). Compared to the average public 4-year college, which charged about $8,893 for in-state tuition for the same academic year (The College Board, 2013), it is easy to see why community colleges are still considered by many to offer a "remarkable bargain" (Bailey, Jaggars, & Jenkins, 2015). The bargain is even more pronounced when considering that the average student (that is, the average student who applies for aid) receives about $4,700 in student financial aid to attend community college (Juszkiewics, 2014).

However—and this is a *big* however—the bargain is more and more often perceived as relative. Because the general historical trend has favored expansion despite static or decreased funding, and because offsetting the expense of expansion through meaning-ful or *substantive* tuition hikes is neither philosophically acceptable nor practical given the student population, community college leaders and administrators have to continually look not only to various means for revenue diversification but to cost reduction measures that will reduce expenditures and better aid efficiency.

Many of these cost-reduction measures have been contro-versial because they include strategies that can pit the priorities of leaders, administrators, and faculty members against the pri-orities of policymakers. For example, the strategies that aim to increase institutional efficiency generally include a marked reliance on adjunct faculty, classrooms with a much larger student-to-faculty ratio, programs that require restrictions in enrollment, and a deeper and more comprehensive reliance on technology.

While the strategies certainly do more with less (and are therefore often politically popular), community college insiders like myself consider such measures to be responsible for expanding community college classrooms with more students and fewer, less qualified (or at least less comprehensively compensated) teachers, or, in the case of expanded technology, with upfront high costs that do not necessarily result in stronger returns. The results of such strategies may save money, but they can also degrade the quality of the education that the colleges offer.

Even more problematic is that measures like these that aim to make community colleges more efficient strengthen a continued adherence to a funding model that generally awards community colleges' resources for enrollment numbers rather than for numbers more strongly associated with performance or outcomes. Such an outdated funding model gives colleges little incentive to ensure that current students achieve high-quality (as in, high-return) goals.

Taken together, the measures that attempt to make the col-leges more efficient and the outdated model supported by such measures simply augment the cafeteria-style culture that Bailey,

Jaggars, and Jenkins (2015) have roundly and persuasively decried as a complete failure. Although such efforts are widely practiced, they usually prove inadequate to either significantly improving a college's bottom line or significantly improving student outcomes. They are therefore precisely the kinds of strategies that suggest that the bargain offered by community colleges is in fact only relative.

Take, for example, the aforementioned reliance on adjunct and part-time faculty. Because they are considerably cheaper to employ than unionized full-time faculty, adjuncts and part-timers have over the years become a larger and larger presence on community college campuses. In 2011, adjuncts and part-time faculty generally made up 49 percent of community colleges' instructional staff (Kena et al., 2015).

Adjuncts and part-timers are certainly qualified, and they offer community colleges a departmental flexibility and comprehensiveness that the colleges would not otherwise be able to claim. However, these instructors do not usually receive the kinds of support or salary that would allow them to foster the developmental environment required by so many of our students. In fact, the overwhelming reliance on adjuncts probably detains the progress of the majority of students who necessitate precisely the holistic approach to student support for which I advocate (Jenkins & Rodriguez, 2013).

∼

The most popular measures for increasing the efficiency of community college institutions are also controversial because it simply is not clear if *efficiency* per se is a goal that community colleges have failed to meet (Belfield & Jenkins, 2014). At the same time that appropriations for community colleges fell (from 1987 to 2008), so too did community college expenditures (Belfield & Jenkins, 2014).

The lower expenditures resulted from some significant cuts, and significant cuts resulted—unsurprisingly—in lower outputs. The culmination of cuts in appropriations, cuts in expenditures, and cuts in outcomes has meant that community colleges have tended toward a "lower-quality, but cheaper" education rather than the "higher-quality, but no more expensive" education that would enable the sector—and its students—to thrive.

The tendency for more-but-not-necessarily-better has also been buttressed by the funding that takes its cues from enrollment rather than performance. While the model made sense in the 1960s, when providing a much wider access to higher education was absolutely paramount to supplying the social progress and equality that so many Americans demanded, it may no longer make sense. To better balance the historical emphasis on access, the colleges instead need to refocus efforts on achievement. If the model for funding appropriations continues to privilege numbers of students over higher quality outcomes, such a balance cannot be achieved. In fact, if institutions are effective in enhancing their retention rates while maintaining their recruitment efforts, the population of students will *increase*. This will create problems of physical capacity and increased need for state and local funding.

Indeed, for *efficiency* to be a meaningful term for community colleges, it cannot just refer to appropriations and expenditures. It must also and emphatically refer to higher quality outcomes for students and thus for society. Such efficiency should enable community college students to be able to contribute to increased revenues for the colleges. But such efficiency should also allow community college students to make a far more substantive case that they offer a high return on community investment.

∽

It is clear that as we look ahead to developing new solutions to the fiscal challenges faced by our colleges, we must continue to look both outside and inside our institutions' walls. Identifying the means through which to diversify funding and taking advantage of the funding that results from that diversification constitutes an important road to sustainability. Identifying the means through which to make our institutions more efficient *without sacrificing educational quality* constitutes another.

Given the precarious nature of state and local funding, and given the need to maintain low tuitions, it is imperative to find economically viable ways to fund entry-level initiatives like enhanced academic advisement and enhanced support services. We must take advantage of the revenues that each student brings to the institution. Perhaps it is best to conclude this chapter with a hypothetical illustration of how we can fund these initiatives.

Let us assume that community college X has an enrollment of 8000 FTE (full-time enrolled) students. Let us also assume the tuition paid by a full-time student taking 12 credits is $3,500 and that the state and the county contribute $4,000 per full-time equivalent student. The annual revenue budget for this college is therefore $60,000,000. Further, let's assume that the operating expenses for this institution total 59 million dollars. This creates a reserve of 1 million dollars a year so long as the enrollment is sustained. If this institution has a retention rate from fall to fall of 68 percent, this means that the institution has to bring in 2,560 FTEs new students per year. Any dip in enrollment has a direct impact on the operating budget and on the reserves.

As I pointed out above, fluctuations in enrollments are common. However, if the retention rate increases to 80 percent from fall to fall, and the new student enrollment remains steady at 2,560 FTEs, the total enrollment increases to 8,960 FTEs, which generates an annual operating budget of $67,200,000. Assuming a requirement of 1 million dollars in reserves, this leaves 5 million dollars per year for new investments.

Increasing retention is how a fiscally prudent administration can fund the innovations described in Chapter 3. However, the board of trustees and the president of the college must prepare the public and the legislature to sustain this increase in revenues. In the hypothetical illustration, 960 new FTEs would cost the county and the state $3,840,000. This is no small amount for a college in a small municipality. However, if the graduation rate increases from 18 percent (1,440) to 30 percent (2,400), and 50 percent of the graduating class increases their earning by $10,000 per year because of the associate's degree and are taxed at a rate of 6.6 percent ($312,000), the state and the county would recoup their investment in less than three years and would make much more over the lifetime of the employees. This is the bulk of the campaign that must be mounted.

The student-centered model *can be funded.* Community college leaders and administrators must work to ensure that the impact on the tax base produced by graduates is made known to community members, business owners, philanthropic organizations, officials, policymakers, and private donors. We must pursue all federal, business, private, and philanthropic avenues to ensure financial stability. We must identify the most reasonable means by which to ensure economic efficiency. We must build alliances with the business community, city or county planners, and elected officials. We must make it widely known that community colleges are a crucial component of the economic welfare of society. Only by shoring up the financial viability of our institutions can we enact the student-centered transformation that will allow our schools to make good on their promises and fulfill their democratic potential.

Chapter 6

A Brighter Future

Institutional, Administrative, Faculty, and Student Development

The community college of the future undoubtedly has much to accomplish. It must actuate its promise to offer both wide access and attainable achievement. It must also take its rightful place as a crucial institution in America's postsecondary system and in the global economy. The community college of the future must aim high for tomorrow so as to position itself to radically and comprehensively improve the institution today. As leaders, administrators, faculty members, and policymakers, we must do our significant part to enact this shift. By working to mend the promise extended on behalf of our institutions, by keeping our doors open and substantially improving the high quality education we provide, we ensure that our institutions come closer than ever to fulfilling our democratic mandate.

To reinvigorate our institutional promise and safeguard our institutional relevance in the twenty-first century, to enact the transformation of our schools into student-centered institutions where pedagogy and support services are informed by an abiding culture of care, and to secure stable funding into the indeterminate future, our schools must demonstrate an incredible institutional will to succeed. We can begin to do this through developing strong leaders, educating capable administrators, preparing and supporting faculty members, and welcoming and working to develop *all* of our students.

To work to this end, we can no longer afford to assume that effective leaders, administrators, and faculty are born. We must instead recognize that much like successful students, consistently impactful personnel and support staff are *fostered*. They are provided ample opportunities for professionalization. They are offered avenues for continued education, development, and support.

In fact, effective community colleges are effective because they are staffed and taught by administrators and faculty members who receive an extension of the type of hands-on guidance from which our students so benefit. These administrators and faculty members are fully supported in their efforts—both inside and outside the institution and the classroom—to ensure that they are able to extend to students the opportunities and individualized help that students need to reach their personal and professional goals.

To execute the changes that I advocate throughout this book, our institutions must ensure that at each administrative level—from the president and administrative leaders to the student support staff—our personnel are ready and able to embody the promise of our schools. Obviously, a strong leader can help to make this happen. A top-down approach is certainly no guarantee of success (and is sometimes a major obstruction), but enabling staff- and faculty-wide embodiment of the community college promise will only happen on a comprehensive level through radical acts on the part of leaders and presidents.

Of course, one aggressive initiative is not enough. As Joshua Wyner argues in *What Excellent Community Colleges Do* (2014), an institution cannot reap the benefits of the sort of sweeping change that positively impacts students and institutions through one bold action. Rather, the sort of sweeping change for which I advocate, which absolutely includes big shifts in culture and attitude, depends on comprehensive initiatives aimed at transforming our institutions from the inside out.

To build institutional will, leaders and presidents must first work to procure a comprehensive commitment on the part of all institutional supporters. Sometimes leaders and presidents must make difficult decisions to gain the commitment. In fact, Wyner suggests, and I too have observed, that the best and most successful community college leaders do not rely on empty platitudes and expect change to follow. Instead, successful community colleges' leaders take meaningful and multi-directional steps toward implementing impactful change.

To my mind, altering our community colleges so that they are more holistically informed by an actionable culture of care means adopting strong new approaches to business-as usual. An important step that leaders, administrators, and faculty members can take is to shift our collective understanding of business-as-usual to accommodate a far more businesslike approach. At first glance, adopting a more professional culture may appear to run counter to the more traditional workings of educational institutions, and administrators and faculty members may resist such a change. Leaders may have to advocate for a businesslike culture through substantive actions. Wyner, for instance, argues (2014) for closing down persistently ineffective programs and for firing or facilitating the retirement of faculty and staff members who are clearly apathetic to the community college mission or who demonstrate an obvious lack of commitment to college and/or student success.

In some ways, Wyner's advice flies in the face of the comprehensive culture of care for which I have so thoroughly argued throughout this book. However, his point is an important one. It is challenging indeed to re-vision an institution dedicated to cultivating learning and potential among disparate student populations as a more efficient, perhaps more utilitarian institution that secures deliverables through a specific and accountable culture of care. But if community colleges are to become student-centered institutions dedicated to mending and enacting an institutional promise of access and achievement, this is exactly the kind of shift that must occur.

The seeds of the kind of radical change so necessary for our institutions cannot flourish in imbalanced soil. Indeed, the institutional transformation that I describe throughout this book depends on community college leaders caring enough to ensure that *all* members of the institution, including administrative staff, faculty members, student support personnel, and the students themselves, feel that their work is an effective, meaningful part of a functioning whole. This can begin to happen when community college leaders are able to ensure that all programs and all personnel within the community college's purview are functional and contributory to our common goal.

Carefully cultivating institutional offerings is important, but it is in no way enough to promote comprehensive, inside-out change. Therefore, colleges must augment a more businesslike approach with a far more comprehensive effort toward developing and supporting staff and faculty. When staff and faculty feel unsupported, unrecognized, and unrewarded, they cannot contribute to the positive change required for our students and our institutions to succeed. To obtain a college-wide commitment to renew the community college promise, community college leaders and presidents must therefore foster excellent, dedicated administrators and support staff.

~

If my long tenure in community colleges has taught me one thing, it is that excellent administrators and support staff are the drivers of a healthy community college culture. In fact, exceptional community colleges are often exceptional because a comprehensively functional and competent administration works behind the scenes to enable the advancement of the college's students. Although not all of these administrators provide direct or hands-on services to students, they routinely ensure that those services are easily executable for others who are better positioned to provide them.

Accordingly, it is important that community college leaders routinely recognize that excellent community college administrators and support staff, while not necessarily rare specimens, differ substantively from their less effective colleagues, and in some important ways. Community college leaders must be able to determine the difference so as to develop the values they want to see reflected in their institutions. By fostering a competent staff dedicated to excellence, community college leaders go a long way toward preparing institutions for broader, sustained success.

Of course, preparing such a staff is not necessarily straight-forward: it depends on a observational keenness and the awareness that what makes an excellent and effective administrator in one organization may not always seamlessly translate to another. This is particularly true in the case of our schools. Unlike other organizations, including more traditional 4-year schools, community colleges require a specific, but also specifically broad skillset. Given the argument I've delivered through this book, this should come as no surprise. I've already shown that our institutions and our students differ in some significant ways from other postsecondary schools and students. Naturally, our administrators are different, too.

Excellent community college administrators are excellent at precisely those things that make our institutions—and our institutional culture—so special. They are defined by their ability to demonstrate deep and nuanced understanding of our student populations, including the sometimes-startling diversity that characterizes and sometimes divides these student populations. Excellent community college administrators are also defined by their demonstrable commitment to our colleges' missions. Such a commitment is not superficial. Instead, excellent community college administrators are professionally devoted to our colleges and are willing to serve as what I think of as "servant leaders," after Greenleaf and Spears (1998). These administrators are poised to guide students and engage with colleagues. They are also willing and able to meaningfully contribute to the institution's wider community, as well.

～

The leadership component of "servant leaders" is just as crucial as the service component. If identifying excellent community college administrators is difficult, identifying excellent community college *leaders* from among these administrators is even more challenging. Today, this difficulty is pressing because a school's institutional culture so often depends on its leaders. Indeed, according to the Achieving the Dream National Reform Network and The Aspen Institute (2013) "every high performing community college has a first-rate president" (p. 2).

Reports from the American Association of Community Colleges (2005) note that the current generation of leaders is graying and that many community college leaders are set to retire. We must therefore identify, and quickly, the next generation of leadership. Although the process for ensuring that qualified, dedicated, and capable candidates take the place of effective presidents is far from straightforward (*Hiring Exceptional Community College Presidents*, 2014), I believe that we can identify the next generation of leaders by fostering our current administrators. In fact, community college leaders can be identified by the same skillset required for excellent administrators, especially that aforementioned willingness to work as servant leaders.

According to Margaret Lee (2014), retired President of Oakton Community College in Illinois, the skillsets required for administrative leadership are often rooted in the classroom: "academic competencies are the essential vocational competencies" (p. 23). The best and most effective community college leaders and administrators therefore communicate fluently with all levels of administration, faculty, students, policymakers, community members, and business interests and leaders. They demonstrate critical, information, and technological literacy. They possess analytical and evaluative abilities and are regularly able to solve complex problems, usually within the context of a team.

Effective administrative leaders also possess budgeting, management, and lobbying skills. They are able to engage in relationship building and in the types of fund- and friendraising that I described in previous chapters. Excellent administrative leaders show a general willingness to meet ongoing demands for accountability, and they are open to change—not just administrative change but curricular, pedagogical change, and cultural change, as well. They are able to consistently promote the community college promise of wide access and navigable paths to achievement, and they are willing to take risks for the benefit of the institutions and its students. Excellent community college administrators demonstrate a clarity (but also a flexibility) of purpose and, perhaps above all, the active willingness to listen to others at the institution and in the community.

While this list of professional competencies is undeniably long, I can put the requirements yet another way. Excellent community college administrators possess the seeds of leadership: they are able to embody and communicate the competencies they want to see reflected in the institutions they represent and in the students they serve.

Ultimately, gifted administrators possess a combination of talent and hard work, and are able to take advantage of every pertinent opportunity. They stand apart and are often incredibly memorable. In fact, I well remember working with gifted administrator Matthew Goldstein. When he became Chancellor of the City University of New York in 1999, CUNY was a disorganized second-class system of approximately 17 campuses. Goldstein knew it well because he had served as president, first at Baruch College in CUNY and then at Adelphi University. Additionally, when he took the position of Chancellor of CUNY, he was the first chancellor who was also an alumnus of one of its colleges—City College.

Goldstein was a gifted administrator, and he came with a mandate. The Board of Trustees, led by Herman Badillo, had appointed Goldstein shortly after the controversial release of Mayor Giuliani's Advisory Task Force report, "The City University of New York: An Institution Adrift." Goldstein was appointed to implement the recommendations contained in the report, including designating two senior colleges, "flagship institutions," to attract high-performing students; providing "separate, additional financing for students needing remedial instruction," so that students did not use up their aid while acquiring skills they should have gained prior to college; consolidating remedial courses at community colleges and implementing better testing; and working with area high schools to raise secondary-school standards (Mayor's Advisory Task Force, 1999).

Goldstein's successful implementation of the system's transformation depended on his ability to clearly state the parameters of change. He established clear lines of communication with colleagues and subordinates. His excellent communication skills also enabled him to develop a trusting relationship with the Board of

Trustees. During his tenure, Goldstein was able to implement all of the recommendations contained in the controversial report. He was able to accomplish the task because he possessed so many of the skills that make for an excellent leader, including a firm hand and an ability to clearly articulate needs. Among his many accomplishments, he implemented a set of accountability measures that made each of the campus presidents accountable for the operations of their institutions. He was respectful of the campus presidents and was therefore able to manage a disparate system in an elegant and effective manner.

Effective leadership demands a deep understanding of an institution's mission and an unwavering commitment to it. Servant leadership means positioning the needs of the institution well above any individual leader. An *effective servant leader* is honest, forthright, and decisive. Matthew Goldstein possessed all of these characteristics. Thanks to his gifts, City University is a far different place today than it was twenty years ago, and its national reputation continues to grow. The stakeholders are keenly aware of the system's importance, and the trust has resulted in generous funding by the city and state.

I have also had the opportunity to work with a similarly supportive chancellor. During my brief tenure at Bronx Community College, I had the privilege of working with the new Chancellor of the City University of New York, James Milliken. What immediately struck me about his administrative style was his inclusiveness of individual campus presidents. He approached the leadership of CUNY by establishing partnerships with campus presidents as well as with the rest of the chancellery.

Milliken's ability to engender trust among the campus presidents has already begun to yield positive results. While no one doubts that he has the power to determine the direction of the entire system, campus presidents also trust that he will not exercise personal power unless it becomes absolutely necessary. With Milliken's help, the new agenda for CUNY is being formulated from the inside, with the advice and consent of the stakeholders. This signifies the system's maturity. Like Goldstein, Milliken came to CUNY at the right time. He has taken advantage of broad support and been able to bolster the lot of the community colleges and establish a new medical school. His leadership is infectious and, speaking from my own experience, campus presidents cannot help but to emulate it.

Both Goldstein and Milliken show that servant leaders adapt to the requirements of the institution. An effective servant leader meets the institution wherever it is in its development. For example, an institution in crisis may need a strong hand. A more mature institution may need more inclusiveness, more trusting relationships, and greater teamwork. Each leader must assess the status of the institution that they lead before accepting the position. The board of trustees is instrumental in laying the foundation for a good match. A good fit depends on the consonance between the stage of development of the institution and the style of the administrator. Indeed, a well-run institution has all of its key positions filled by the "right" individuals. This is the difficult task of leading complex enterprises such as the universities and colleges.

$$\sim$$

Given the lengthy list of qualifications and the relatively few effective servant leaders, it is no wonder that community colleges are challenged in the routine identification of excellent administrators and support staff. It is all but impossible to uniformly staff an institution—any institution—with competent, effective, excellent administrators at each and every level. Despite the challenges, however, our institutions *can* begin to foster this kind of administrative excellence. We cannot do this by assuming that leaders possess the innate mark of command and therefore rise efficiently through the ranks; nor can we assume that our colleges will always be successful at identifying, hiring, and procuring the very best candidates. Most of us who work in community colleges are well aware that the process of bringing on highly successful administrators can often be arduous, difficult to streamline, and challenging to replicate through straightforward delegation.

We must therefore recognize that the individuals who will become excellent administrative staff and excellent leaders are usually those individuals already dedicated to our institutions, our missions, and our students. They already serve our schools. However, and much like our students, they need to be provided with a clearer path by which to fully develop their skills. Community colleges can provide this path with effective professionalization opportunities, including opportunities for continued education, leadership development, and consistent, meaningful support.

Of course, many community colleges already offer development opportunities for administrators and staff. But such programs are often too informal or too limited in terms of scope or longevity. They are also often narrowed in terms of which administrators and staff can participate. It is imperative that we expand development opportunities for all staff members; the comprehensive development and support that is so crucial to our students is also crucial to the future of our schools. By committing resources to providing the development and support services that are often available in other customer-serving industries, we ensure that our current administrators become the administrators we want—and need—to be the future servant leaders of our institutions.

I believe that it is the job of every community college to extend the culture of care with which the institution supports its students to its professional and faculty level. We must provide specific and structured opportunities for professional education, development, and support if we want to generate leaders among our ranks.

~

Professional education must therefore happen at every level, but to more quickly enact a widespread cultural transformation into student-centered institutions, our schools must first focus on providing education and development opportunities for frontline student support staff. These are the staff members who represent our schools to potential students and to the community. These are therefore the staff members who must also be, in accordance with Wyner's point (2014), exceedingly comfortable in a business-like environment.

Simply put, frontline student support staff must be given the education and development opportunities necessary to learn and practice the tools by which to execute excellent customer relationships. This of course depends on the recognition among current leaders and administrators that incoming students should be considered more like the clients they are than the supplicants they are deemed to be in more traditional pedagogical modes.

I have frequently observed that without the education and support necessary to initiate and sustain a more businesslike culture, a college's administrative staff too easily becomes an impediment rather than an on-ramp to student success. This was the case with Jamie, described in Chapter 3. Jamie sought an avenue for help at the bursar's office, but she was informed that she had reached a dead end. While it is most certainly not always the case, too many students at the schools I've served have had to fight too hard to receive the services they need to succeed. Frontline personnel *must* be given the education and the support that will enable them to work as institutional facilitators, not as sentries.

Institutions can create professional education opportunities to this end. Just as we know that our students benefit from entry-level orientation (Best Practices, 2014; Mullendore & Banahan, 2005), we can assume that our administrators and frontline personnel will, too. Community college should therefore offer comprehensive orientation opportunities that introduce incoming administrators and staff to the college's student populations, missions, culture, and role in the community.

Unlike our students, however, administrators and student support staff, particularly frontline support staff, must be educated as both mentors and managers. They must consequently be provided with ample and deep instruction on the import of establishing and maintaining excellent relationships with students, with colleagues, and with community members, too. It is, after all, through these relationships that we enact the culture of care that supports our students, sustains our professional environment, and makes the continual and strong case for our institutional relevance.

Such instruction must account for the complexity of students and institutions. For example, it is not enough to educate frontline student support staff in easing students' transition from high-school graduate or highly trained worker or baccalaureate-aspirant or recent retiree to postsecondary *student*. Instead, and as I've indicated in previous chapters, community college administrators and student support staff, positions that include entry-level advisors and success coaches, must *also* be provided with ample training opportunities in interviewing students and in detecting the areas of both strengths and weaknesses that are routinely missed by assessment exams (to take but two examples).

This will absolutely require a more holistic and more persistent program for professional education. In fact, I envision a program that makes use of institutional resources, including the incomparably comprehensive faculty that staffs our colleges. Who better to help provide opportunities for administrative education than faculty members specially trained in those fields?

Indeed, administrators and frontline support staff who are able to understand the curriculum and pedagogies in their departments are also able to work closely and effectively with faculty members. The collaboration is crucial for implementing the academic teams I describe in Chapter 4. But it is also critical for developing more comprehensive and widely applicable benchmarks for student progress and for determining the warning signs that indicate student distress. By building connections between administrative staff and faculty members around student concerns, we help to activate the complementary, intrusive support services for which I advocate. We also build a stronger foundation for inside-out institutional transformation.

Of course, professional education cannot stop at administrative-level orientation and faculty alignment. Community college support staff must also be encouraged to (and must be able to) engage in career-long opportunities through which staff can continue refining professional competencies. Examples of this type of development might be in the form of encouraging or even requiring interdepartmental internship engagements. It might also be in structuring longstanding mentorships between more senior and more junior administrative and support staff.

Continuing development opportunities might also take the form of establishing comprehensive release time protocols. While such protocols are often available to full-time faculty members at more traditional 4-year colleges, administrators and support staff at community colleges can also benefit from participating in workshops, conferences, or continuing education opportunities that are outside the institution but nonetheless relevant to their work. Continuing development opportunities might also take the form of the promotion of and facilitation of working groups. Such groups, again often the purview of full-time faculty, open an arena in which diverse administrative and support staff members can engage in and share relevant research and continuing education experiences.

Basically, by building and advancing strategies to more substantively educate, develop, and support community colleges' administrators and support staff, extant community college leaders ensure both the introduction and the ultimate perpetuation of the institutional culture we want enacted for and among our students. Through these opportunities, we implement the strategies that allow every member of the community college staff to embody and thus communicate and deliver our promises to students and the wider community.

While certainly time-consuming and occasionally costly, today's community college leaders must implement these strategies for future security. Much like the intrusive support offered through programs like ASAP, creating professional development opportunities for administration and student support staff will ultimately prove cost-effective. Through these opportunities, we deliver our culture of care, ensure the stability of our staff, and expand the pool of community college leaders who will be prepared to deliver our institutional promise during the twenty-first century.

⁓

While the need for professional education, development, and support at the administration level is undoubtedly important, it must be matched by attention to the education, development, and support necessary for part- and full-time faculty members. Unfortunately, too many community colleges today lack broad and deep professionalization opportunities for administrative and support staff *and* for part- and full-time faculty members.

There are, of course, good logistical reasons for the lack of systemic support. In the case of faculty members, cohesive professional development is challenging to implement because so many of our teachers are part-time, adjunct, or so-called "contingent" faculty. The reliance on part-time or adjunct faculty is necessary from a fiscal standpoint, and part-time faculty often go a long way toward ensuring the economic viability of contemporary community colleges. However, the increased dependence on part-time faculty members also represents a major problem for our colleges.

As I briefly indicated in Chapter 4, these faculty members are emphatically *not* a problem because they lack the skills, ability, or commitment to deliver appropriate and responsive pedagogy to our students—they don't. They are also emphatically *not* a problem because they are less committed to our students, our missions, or our institutions—they are often just as and sometimes even more committed than full-time faculty. Rather, part-time faculty, no matter how passionate, no matter how engaged, no matter how dedicated, still exist apart from the institutional culture at most community colleges.

According to a report by the Coalition on the Academic Workforce (2012), part-time and adjunct faculty members are often plentiful but are infrequently integrated into the current iteration of the community college institutional culture. Through far lower rates of compensation, few if any benefits, and a lack of an institutional home, such as an office or sometimes even a desk, these contingent teachers are implicitly (and sometimes explicitly) marginalized by the institution.

I am of course not alone in recognizing the major disconnect (Center for Community College Engagement, 2014; Fain, 2014; Pearch & Marutz, 2005). Part-time, adjunct, or contingent faculty members increasingly constitute the majority of the faculty members who teach our students. Yet they continue to remain nonintegrated members of our institutions and are not extended the same privileges—including opportunities for professionalization and continuing education—that are often offered to full-time faculty members.

Because community college funding will likely continue to be unstable and even scarce into the indeterminate future, it is improbable that the institutional reliance on part-time faculty will be rolled back any time soon. Community college leaders must therefore find a place for these faculty members—again, the majority of our teachers—in the institutional culture we want to create.

For example, we must ensure that part-time faculty members receive the same training, the same professionalization opportunities, and the same opportunities for support as the rest of our faculty and staff. Indeed, without offering these teachers—and it bears repeating that these are the majority of faculty members employed by most community colleges—the same opportunities for training, professionalization, and support, we cannot expect to enact the institutional transformation that will reach our students.

To start, part-time, adjunct, or contingent faculty should be included in the same orientation sessions often available to full-time faculty. Like the orientation sessions offered to incoming administrators and support staff, meaningful orientation sessions will include comprehensive education on students and missions. For part-time faculty members, however, a meaningful orientation will also include straightforward logistical information about institutional practicalities that longstanding faculty and staff members take for granted. Supplying incoming teachers with this knowhow signals the institutional acceptance of the legitimacy of their work.

Without access to orienting information, part-time faculty will continue to operate on the margins of our schools. To bring them further into our institutional fold, we must also structure mentoring relationship between new and returning part-time faculty members and part-time and full-time faculty members. In addition, part-time faculty members should be provided with information regarding a clear career path forward. Not every part-time faculty member will qualify for full-time work, but every part-time faculty member should be able to take on increased responsibilities and engage in the continuing education that can put them on the path to more stable job opportunities.

Part-time faculty members must also be encouraged, perhaps through the aforementioned implementation of clear release time protocols, to engage in and share research at conferences and colloquia. They must also be incentivized to participate in working groups or structured roundtable discussions. This will cost additional upfront resources, but it will pay great dividends in retention and development.

All of these efforts, many of which are far less costly than may be imagined (Fain, 2014; Kezar & Maxey, 2013) constitute substantive ways in which we can ensure that our part-time faculty members are made to feel as protected and empowered by our culture of care as are our students. If part-time faculty members continue to feel (and to often actually be) marginalized, they are far more likely to sustain the sense of marginalization that adheres so persistently to both our institutions and our students.

∾

The prevalence of part-time faculty and the dearth of extant institutional support mechanisms for them constitute one major reason for the lack of comprehensive or otherwise systemic support. However, the overextension of current full-time faculty members constitutes another major challenge to cohesive or comprehensive professional development.

Full-time faculty members are not usually tasked with teaching as many courses (or as many remedial or developmental courses) as part-time faculty members. But full-time faculty members are often the first in line for taking on expanded roles. They are frequently required to substantively participate on academic teams, to help implement research-based pedagogies, and to work quickly and efficiently to integrate technology-enhanced coursework. In fact, both full-time faculty roles will be expanded even further when the changes for which I advocate are put into place.

Consequently, full-time faculty must also be supported in their efforts through the same kinds of mechanisms I describe above. The difference in these mechanisms must be the recognition among community college leaders and administrators that full-time community college faculty members are often under different pressures than those faced by either their part-time community college counterparts or their full-time counterparts at more traditional 4-year schools.

Whereas faculty at 4-year institutions engage in discipline-specific conferences, seminars, or colloquia to further their professional development, engage in continuing education, and seek professional support, full-time faculty at community colleges are often preoccupied with exercising an already incredibly comprehensive skillset. In addition to their academic, pedagogical, and research specialties, full-time faculty at community colleges are also often involved in larger institutional concerns, such as community outreach, and in both formal and informal student advising.

Consequently, the opportunities for professional development, education, and support that must be made available for full-time faculty must address highly specific academic, institutional, and student specific issues. Subjects appropriate for inclusion in development programs might be topics on advisement strategies, student assessment, and program requirements. Subjects could be offered through certificate programs whereby rewards are disbursed upon successful completion, or perhaps skills could be gained through conferences, seminars, and colloquia that allow faculty members the opportunity to gain new skills while also showcasing their own pedagogical specialties or research interests.

≈

Of course, making professional education and development opportunities available is just an initial step toward implementing broad support for community college faculty members. There are in fact a host of other difficulties associated with implementing these education and development opportunities. To take but one example, current community college leaders must work incredibly hard to structure opportunities so that they fit within staff and faculty members' very busy, very variable schedules.

Simply finding common times for faculty members to engage in extracurricular activities represents a major challenge. Many of our schools' teachers, sometimes both part- and full-time staff, *already* teach four or five courses *and* engage in some sort of advising, service learning, or other community service. Additionally, teaching times can be so variable (this is particularly true when including part-time faculty schedules and when accounting for the unconventional times at which technologically enhanced courses are often taught) that finding consonant meeting times becomes a Herculean task.

In addition to the challenges associated with scheduling and the difficulties in asking already committed faculty members to pry open their calendars, there are the challenges associated with the money that might be required to participate in off-campus events. Release protocols can smooth institutional logistics, but such agreements only very rarely provide a means for covering the extraneous costs of participating in the opportunities for continuing education and support available through conferences and workshops.

The obstacles can be formidable, but rewarding development opportunities can be successfully offered to part- and full-time faculty. I have been lucky enough to see it myself. When I was a young associate dean at Borough Manhattan Community College, I was able to participate in the Harvard Institute for Educational Management. The City University of New York selected one representative from the 4-year colleges and one representative from the community colleges to participate in this important professional development activity. In this particular instance, I was selected and able to learn about management techniques that heretofore I was completely unaware of. I firmly believe that it is because of this training that I became a community college president.

Professional help is not relegated to already established programs. When I was president of Queensborough Community College I established a Center for Excellence in Teaching and Learning. The safe environment provided by the Center resulted in many pedagogical innovations; among them were the high-impact activities for the Queensborough Academies. When I became interim president of Bronx Community College, I used the already established Center for Excellence in Teaching and Learning as a vehicle to promulgate my pedagogical philosophy. I conducted a series of seminars where I interacted with all members of the college community. I believe that this activity was very useful for staff to understand the direction of my presidency. These faculty-oriented activities solidified my standing with the academic community. Hopefully, some of the attendees will carry on with the institutional transformation that I worked to achieve.

Community colleges can absolutely foster the faculty members who will enable institutional transformation, but we need them to be able to display the institutional will. Luckily, my experience has shown me that our faculty members are some of the most passionate, most dedicated, and most pedagogically active teachers in the postsecondary system. Like me, they may enter our institutions because they see community college as a steppingstone. They may, like me, become inspired by our students and deeply invested in our missions and our promise. They often choose to stay, like I did, because they want to be part of a scaled effort dedicated to enacting meaningful social change.

∼

Administration, support staff, and faculty members are one—admittedly big—piece of the community college of the future.

Our institution will rely heavily on this cohort to enact its transformation. However, the community college of the future must be able to do a bit more. In addition to building a demonstrable institutional will among leaders, administrators, and faculty members, current community college leaders must also work to build institutional will among our students. Success in the long-term depends on the effective implementation of the student support services that I described in Chapters 3 and 4, but success also depends on providing the staged development of softer skills that will facilitate our students' commitment to and achievement within our schools.

First, our students must receive some of the same sort of entry-level opportunities for development as administrative staff and faculty. While these opportunities generally fall under the purview of entry-level support services I've previously described, they must also include a frank communication of what might be called intangibles.

For example, in order to be able to work committedly at our institutions, students must be able to apprehend their role as a *student within* our institutions. They therefore must learn institutional expectations at the outset of their studies, and be made aware of the institutional resources that can enable them to meet these expectations. In the process of understanding their important role within our schools, students must be given concrete examples of expectations and be allowed and enabled to practice different strategies for meeting these expectations.

Second, students must be incentivized on their way to award or degree completion. A more traditionalist view may hold that graduation should be its own reward. However, in the current community college milieu, where paths toward achievement are generally obscured, and where students can toil until their aid runs dry and yet be no closer to their personal or professional goals, students should at least be cognizant of the progress they make toward completion or graduation.

Student progress can and should be marked by milestones. Rather than pushing recognition and celebration to a traditional terminal point, milestones enable recognition of the *process* toward a goal that may still be in the distance. Common milestones might include recognition or celebration for reaching a certain number of credits (12, 30, or 45, for example). They might include recognition or celebration for progress toward an academic goal, such as completing 50 percent of a program's requirements. Or they might include completion of separate terminal certificates, such as an ESL certificate.

In addition to marking important progress, milestones can also be used by the institution as helpful data points. Determining which students achieve milestones and when they do so can impact student support services. In fact, research indicates that the earlier students reach a milestone, the more likely they are to achieve their academic goals (Calcagno, Crosta, Bailey, & Jenkins, 2006).

Third, students will also benefit from development opportunities that usher them out of community colleges and into the target environment of their future educational or professional goals. Etiquette workshops, interview training, resume writing, job placement fairs, and on-the-spot admissions to baccalaureate-granting colleges show our students that our institutions are not only relevant to their needs and their goals, but are radically committed to supporting them every step of the way.

This is how we procure the institutional will to transform our schools. By showing our staff, our faculty members, and our students that we care deeply about the institutional promise of wide access and navigable paths of achievement; that we are capable of establishing the practices that make our promise actionable; and that we are willing to provide the opportunities that give our staff, faculty members, and students the ability to partake in institutional success; we take a crucial first step toward enacting our institution's democratic potential.

Epilogue

Can America's community colleges fulfill the promise of universal access and excellent completion rates? I believe that the answer is unequivocally yes. In this book we have examined the development of community colleges, we have described the transformation that is needed in order to convert comprehensive community colleges into student-oriented institutions, and we have described how we can finance this transformation. We have also explored the leadership qualities that are necessary to effectuate this transformation.

Community colleges are a different type of institution; they straddle the boundary between the secondary and tertiary sector of education. The size of the community college student population and their importance in creating a well-educated and well-trained workforce make community colleges paramount to American society. Yet these colleges are generally misunderstood. The public tends to see them as way stations for those who do not belong in college; taxpayers tend to see them as a drain of public treasure; and the students themselves tend to minimize the importance of attending these institutions. Further, skeptics see community colleges as a form of educational welfare.

This book is an attempt to correct this notion. Once we understand how community colleges operate, once we understand that these colleges cannot simply emulate baccalaureate-granting colleges, once we understand that these colleges must be a combination of academic institutions and social agencies, once we understand that successful community colleges must engage in a culture of care, we can create a highly successful system that will meet the goals of its founders by providing universal access with excellent academic results. It is not a hyperbole to state that bolstering community colleges is a matter of national importance.

Bibliography

Achieving the Dream & The Aspen Institute. (2013). *Crisis and opportunity: Aligning the community college presidency with student success*. Retrieved from http://kresge.org

American Association of Community Colleges. (2006). *Competencies for community college leaders*. Washington, DC: American Association of Community Colleges. Retrieved from http://www.aacc.nche.edu

American Association of Community Colleges. (2008). *Funding issues in U.S. community colleges: Findings from a 2007 survey of the national state directors of community colleges*. Washington, DC: American Association of Community Colleges. Retrieved from http://www.aacc.nche.edu/Publications/Pages

American Association of Community Colleges. (2011, April). *The completion agenda: A call to action*. Washington, DC: American Association of Community Colleges. Retrieved from http://www.aacc.nche.edu/Publications/Pages

American Association of Community Colleges. (2011, August). *Report on the 21st-century initiative listening tour*. Washington, DC: American Association of Community Colleges. Retrieved from http://www.aacc.nche.edu/Publications/Pages

American Association of Community Colleges. (2014, January). *Recent national community college enrollment and award completion data*. Washington, DC: American Association of Community Colleges. Retrieved from http://www.aacc.nche.edu/Publications/Pages

American Association of Community Colleges. (2015). *Community college completion: Progress toward 50% increase*. Washington, DC: American Association of Community Colleges. Retrieved from http://www.aacc.nche.edu

American Association of Community Colleges. (2015). *2015 Fact Sheet*. Washington, DC: American Association of Community Colleges. Retrieved from http://www.aacc.nche.edu

American Association of Community Colleges. (2015, November). Relying on Pell. *Data Points*. Washington, DC: American Association of Community Colleges. Retrieved from https://www.aacc.nche.edu

Arum, R., & Roksa, J. (2011). *Academically adrift*. Chicago: University of Chicago Press.

Attewell, P., Lavin, D., Domina, T., & Levey, T. (2006). New evidence on college remediation. *The Journal of Higher Education*, 77(5), 886–924.

Bailey, T. R. (2009, February). *Rethinking developmental education in community college*. (Issue Brief No. 40). New York: Columbia University, Teachers College, Community College Research Center. Retrieved from http://ccrc.tc.columbia.edu

Bailey, T. R., Calcagno, J. J., Jenkins, D., Leinbach, T., & Kienz, G. (2005, June). *Is Student-Right-to-Know all you should know? An analysis of community college graduation rates*. (Working Paper No. 2). New York: Columbia University, Teachers College, Community College Research Center. Retrieved from http://ccrc.tc.columbia.edu

Bailey, T. R., & Cho, S-W. (2010, September). *Developmental education in community colleges*. (CCRC Issue Brief). New York: Columbia University, Teachers College, Community College Research Center. Retrieved from http://ccrc.tc.columbia.edu

Bailey, T. R., Crosta, P. M., & Jenkins, D. (2007). *The value of Student-Right-to-Know data in assessing community college performance*. (CCRC Brief No. 34). New York: Columbia University, Teachers College, Community College Research Center. Retrieved from http://ccrc.tc.columbia.edu

Bailey, T. R., Jaggars, S. S., & Jenkins, D. (2015). *Redesigning community colleges: A clearer path to student success*. Cambridge: Harvard University Press.

Bailey, T. R., Kienzl, G., & Marcotte, D. (2004). *Who benefits from postsecondary occupational training? Findings from the 1980s and 1990s*. (Issue Brief No. 23). New York: Columbia University, Teachers College, Community College Research Center. Retrieved from http://ccrc.tc.columbia.edu

Batten, D. D. (2011). The GI Bill, higher education and American society. *Grove City College Journal of Law and Public Policy*, 2(1), 13–30. Retrieved from http://www2.gcc.edu/orgs/GCLawJournal/?section=archives&page=spring2011

Baum, S., & Ma, J. (2013). *Trends in college pricing*. Washington, DC: The College Board.

Beach, J. M. (2011). *Gateway to opportunity? A history of the community college in the United States*. Sterling, VA: Stylus.

Belfield, C. R., & Jenkins, D. (2014, May–June). Can community colleges continue to do more with less? *Change: The Magazine of Higher Learning*. Retrieved from http://www.changemag.org

Belfield, C. R., & Jenkins, D. (2014). *Community college economics for policymakers: The one big fact and the one big myth* (Working Paper No. 67). New York: Columbia University, Teachers College, Community College Research Center. Retrieved from http://ccrc.tc.columbia.edu

Bensimon, E. M. (2007). The underestimated significance of practitioner knowledge in the scholarship on student success. *The Review of Higher Education*, 30(4), 441–469. Retrieved from http://www.usc.edu

Bers, T. H. (1983). *The promise and reality of women in community colleges*. Paper presented at the conference of the American Educational Research Association, Tempe, AZ. Retrieved from http://files.eric.ed.gov

Blocker, C. E, Plummer, R. H., & Richardson, R. C. (1965). *The two-year college: A social synthesis*. New Jersey: Prentice-Hall.

Bohn, S., Reyes, B., & Johnson, H. (2013, March). *The impact of budget cuts on California's community colleges.* CA: Public Policy Institute of California.

Bragg, D. C. (2001). Community college access, mission, and outcomes: Considering intriguing intersections and challenges. *Peabody Journal of Education,* 76(1), 93–116.

Brock, T. (2010). Young adults and higher education: Barriers and breakthroughs to success. *The Future of Children,* 20(1). 109–132. Retrieved from http://files.eric.ed.gov

Brubacher, J. S., & Rudy, W. (1958). *Higher education in transition: An American history: 1936–1956.* New York: Harper & Row.

Buffington, J. (2003). Learning communities as an instructional model. In M. Orey (Ed.), *Emerging perspectives on learning, teaching, and technology.* Retrieved from http://epltt.coe.uga.edu

Calcagno, J. C., Crosta, P., Bailey, T., & Jenkins, D. (2006). *Stepping stones to a degree: The impact of enrollment pathways and milestones on community college student outcomes.* (CCRC Working Paper No. 4). New York: Columbia University, Teachers College, Community College Research Center. Retrieved from http://files.eric.ed.gov/fulltext/ED494143.pdf

Center for Community College Engagement. (2014). *Contingent commitments: Bringing part-time faculty into focus (a special report from the Center for Community College Engagement).* Austin, TX: The University of Texas at Austin, Program in Higher Education Leadership. Retrieved from http://www.ccsse.org/docs/PTF_Special_Report.pdf

Clark, B. R. (1960). The "cooling-out" function in higher education. *The American Journal of Sociology,* 65(6), 569–576. Retrieved from http://faculty.washington.edu/rsoder/EDUC310/571BurtonClark CoolingOut.pdf

Coalition on the Academic Workforce. (2012, June). *A portrait of part-time faculty members.* (Report). Retrieved from http://www.academicworkforce.org/CAW_portrait_2012.pdf

Cohen, A. M. (2001). Governmental policies affecting community colleges: A historical perspective. In B. Townsend & S. Twombly

(Eds.), *Community colleges: Policy in the future context* (pp. 3–22). Westport, CT: Ablex Publishing.

Cohen, A. M. (2010). *The shaping of American higher education: Emergence and growth of the contemporary system*. (2nd ed.). San Francisco: Jossey-Bass.

Cohen, A .M., Brawer, F. B., & Kisker, C. B. (2014). *The American community college* (6th ed.). San Francisco: Jossey-Bass.

Craig, R. (2015). *College disrupted: The great unbundling of higher education*. New York: Palgrave.

CUNY Working Group on Remediation. (2011, August). *Proposals to improve success rates for students in developmental education at CUNY*. Report of the Working Group on Remediation. New York: CUNY Office of Academic Affairs. Retrieved from http://owl.cuny.edu

Deegan, W. L., & Tillery, D. (1985). *Renewing the American community college*. San Francisco: Jossey-Bass.

Diener, T. (1986). *Growth of an American invention: A documentary history of the junior and community college movement*. New York: Greenwood Press.

Dougherty, K. (1994). *The contradictory college: The conflicting origins, impacts, and futures of the community college*. Albany, NY: State University of New York Press.

Dougherty, K., Bork, R. H., & Natow, R. (2009). *Performance accountability systems for community colleges: Lessons for the voluntary framework of accountability for community colleges*. (Report to the College Board). New York: Columbia University, Teachers College, Community College Research Center. Retrieved from http://ccrc.tc.columbia.edu

Dowd, A. C., & Tong, V. P. (2007). Accountability, assessment, and scholarship of "best practice." In J.C. Smart (Ed.), *Handbook of higher education* (Vol. 22) (pp. 57–119). Dordrecht: Springer.

Eells, W. C. (1931). *The junior college*. Boston: Houghton Mifflin Company.

Engstrom, C., & Tinto, V. (2010). Access without support is not opportunity. *Change: The Magazine of Higher Learning*, 40(1), 46–50.

Fain, P. (2013, May). Low bar, high failure. *Inside Higher Education.* Retrieved from https://www.insidehighered.com

Fain, P. (2014, April). Low expectations, high stakes. *Inside Higher Education.* Retrieved from https://www.insidehighered.com

Fain, P. (2015, February). Living up to the hype. *Inside Higher Education.* Retrieved from https://www.insidehighered.com

Farrell, A. P. (1949). Report of the president's commission: A critical appraisal. *Journal of Educational Sociology, 22*(8), 508–522.

Gabert, G. (1991). *Community colleges in the 1990s.* Bloomington, IN: Phi Delta Kappa Educational Foundation.

Gilbert, C. K., & Heller, D. E. (2013). Access, equity, and community colleges: The Truman Commission and federal higher education policy from 1947 to 2011. *The Journal of Higher Education,* 84(3), 417–443.

Gleazer Jr., E. J. (1980). *The community college: Values, vision, & vitality.* Washington DC: American Association of Community and Junior Colleges.

Gleazer Jr., E. J. (1994). Evolution of junior colleges into community colleges. In G. A. Baker III (Ed.), *A handbook on the community college in America: Its history, mission, and management* (pp. 17–27). Westport, CT: Greenwood Press.

Green, K. C. (1981). Program review and the state responsibility for higher education. *The Journal of Higher Education,* 52(1), 67–80. doi:10.2307/1981153

Greenleaf, R. K., & Spears, L. C. (Eds.). (1998). *The power of servant-leadership.* San Francisco, CA: Berrett-Koehler.

Greenleaf, W. J. (1936). *Junior colleges.* Washington DC: United States Government Printing Office. Retrieved from http://files.eric.ed.gov

Grubb, N. W. (1991). The decline of community college transfer rates: Evidence from national longitudinal surveys. *The Journal of Higher Education,* 62(2), 194–222.

Habley, W. R., & McClanahan, R. (2004). *What works in student retention: Four-year public colleges.* ACT, Inc. Retrieved from https://www.act.org

Hanover Research. (2014, October). *Best practices in retention at community colleges.* (Report). Arlington, VA: Hanover Research,

Academy Administration Practice. Retrieved from http://www.mercedregionalgateway.org

Harper, W. R. (1905). *The trend in higher education*. Chicago: The University of Chicago Press.

Hilgard, E. W. (1882). Progress in agriculture by education and government aid. *The Atlantic Monthly, 49*(294). 531–541. Retrieved from http://dx.doi.org/10.5962/bhl.title.40151

Hiring exceptional community college presidents: Tools for hiring leaders who advance student access and success. (2014). Washington, DC: The Aspen Institute, College Excellence Program. Retrieved from http://www.aspeninstitute.org

Hodara, M., Jaggars, S. S., & Karp, M. M. (2012). *Improving developmental education and placement: Lessons from community colleges across the country*. (Working Paper No. 51). New York: Columbia University, Teachers College, Community College Research Center.

How the GI Bill widened the higher education racial gap. (2003). *The Journal of Blacks In Higher Education*, 41, 36–37.

Hughes, K., & Scott-Clayton, J. (2011). Assessing developmental assessment in community colleges. *Community College Review*, 39(4), 327–351.

Hutcheson, P. A. (2007). The Truman Commission's vision of the future. *Thought & Action: The NEA Higher Education Journal*, Fall, 107–115.

Jaggars, S. S., & Stacey, G. W. (2014, January). *What we know about developmental education outcomes*. (Research Overview). New York: Columbia University, Teachers College, Community College Research Center. Retrieved from http://ccrc.tc.columbia.edu

Jenkins, D., & Rodriguez, O. (2013). Access and success with less: Improving productivity in broad-access postsecondary institutions. *Future of Children*, 23(1), 187–209.

Jenkins, D., Speroni, C., Belfield, C., Jaggars, S. S., & Edgecombe, N. (2010). *A model for accelerating student success of community college remedial English students: Is the Accelerated Learning Program (ALP) effective and affordable?* (CCRC Working Paper No. 21). New York: Columbia University, Teachers College, Community

College Research Center. Retrieved from http://ccrc.tc.columbia. edu

Johnson, N. (2014, April). *College costs, prices and the great recession.* (Lumina Issue Paper). Lumina Foundation. Retrieved from https://www.luminafoundation.org/files/publications/issue_papers/ College_Costs_Prices_and_the_Great_Recession.pdf

Juszkiewicz, J. (2014, April). *Community college students and federal student financial aid: A primer.* Washington DC: American Association of Community Colleges. Retrieved from http://www.aacc.nche.edu

Juszkiewicz, J. (2014). *Recent national community college enrollment and award completion data.* Washington DC: American Association of Community Colleges. Retrieved from http://www.aacc.nche.edu

Kaplan, A. E. (2012). *Voluntary support by type of institution.* Council for Aid to Education. Retrieved from http://cae.org/images/uploads/ pdf/VSE_2012_Sample_Pages.pdf

Karabel, J. (1986). Community colleges and social stratification in the 1980s. *New Directions for Community Colleges, 54,* 13–30.

Karen, D. (1991). The politics of class, race, and gender: Access to higher education in the United States, 1960–1986. *American Journal of Education,* 99(2), 208–237.

Katsinas, S., & Tollefson, T. *Funding issues in U.S. community colleges: Findings from a 2008 survey of the National Council of State Directors of Community Colleges.* (Report). Tuscaloosa, AL: Education Policy Center, The University of Alabama.

Kena, G., Aud, S., Johnson, F., Wang, X., Zhang, J., Rathbun, A., Wilkinson-Flicker, S., & Kristapovich, P. (2014). *The Condition of Education 2014* (NCES 2014-083). Washington, DC: U.S. Department of Education, National Center for Education Statistics. Retrieved from http://nces.ed.gov/pubsearch.

Kena, G., Musu-Gillette, L., Robinson, J., Wang, X., Rathbun, A., Zhang, J., Wilkinson-Flicker, S., Barmer, A., & Dunlop Velez, E. (2015). The Condition of Education 2015 (NCES 2015-144). U.S. Department of Education, National Center for Education Statistics. Washington, DC. Retrieved from http://nces.ed.gov/ pubsearch

Kezar, A., & Maxey, D. (2013). *Dispelling the myths: Resources necessary to support non-tenure-track faculty.* The Delphi Project on the Changing Faculty and Student Success. Retrieved from http://www.uscrossier.org/pullias/wp-content/uploads/2013/10/DelphiProject-Dispelling_the_Myths.pdf

Kim, D., & Rury, J. L. (2007). The changing profile of college access: The Truman Commission and enrollment patterns in the postwar era. *History of Education Quarterly, 47*(3), 302–327.

Kirshstein, R., & Hurlburt, S. (2012). *Revenues: Where does the money come from? A Delta Data Update, 2000–2010.* Washington DC: American Institutes for Research. Retrieved from http://www.deltacostproject.org

Koos, L. V. (1925). *The junior college movement.* Boston: Ginn & Company.

Kozeracki, C., & Brooks, B. (2006). Emerging institutional support for developmental education. In Townsend, B. K. & Dougherty, K. (Eds.), *Community college missions in the 21ˢᵗ century* (pp. 63–73). *New Directions for Community Colleges Series* (Vol. 136). San Francisco: Jossey-Bass.

Land-Grant College Act, 7 U.S.C § 301 (1862). Retrieved from http://www.ourdocuments.gov/doc_large_image.php?doc=33.

Lange, A. F. (1917). The junior college as an integral part of the public school system. *The School Review. 25*(7), 465–479.

Lazerson, M. (1998). The disappointments of success: Higher education after World War II. *Annals of the American Academy of Political and Social Science, 559*, 64–76.

Lee, M. B. (2014). Being a president. In Noreen Thomas (Ed.), *Exploring the Future of Community Colleges* (pp. 23–26). Grand Blanc, MI: Scholar Talk Press. Retrieved from http://www.ferris.edu

Levin, H. M., & Garcia, E. (2012). Cost effectiveness of Accelerated Study in Associate Programs (ASAP) of the City University of New York (CUNY). New York: Columbia University, Teachers College, Center for Benefit-Cost Studies in Education. Retrieved from http://www.nyc.gov

Levin, J., & Kater, S. (Eds.) (2013). *Understanding community colleges.* New York: Routledge.

Luskin, B. (Ed.) (2011). *Legacy of leadership: Profiles of the President of the American Association of Community Colleges, 1958–2010.* Washington, DC: W. K. Kellogg Foundation and American Association of Community Colleges. Retreived from http://www.aacc.nche.edu

Maher, J. (1997). *Mina Shaughnessy: Her life and works.* Urbana: National Council of Teachers.

Marcus, J. (2013, November). Fancy fundraising's new frontier: Community colleges. *Time.* Retrieved from http://nation.time.com

Martorana, S. V. (1974). State-level planning for community colleges: Are the 1202 commissions a centripetal or centrifugal force in postsecondary education? *Essays on Education* 4, 1–17.

Mayor's Advisory Task Force on the City University of New York. (1999, June). *The City University of New York: An institution adrift.* Retrieved from http://www.nyc.gov

McCarton, A. M. (1983). The community college mission: Present challenges and future visions. *The Journal of Higher Education,* 54(6), 676–692.

McPhail, C. J., & McPhail, I. P. (2006). Prioritizing community college missions: A directional effort. In Townsend, B.K. & Dougherty, K. (Eds.), *Community college missions in the 21ˢᵗ century* (pp. 91–99). *New Directions for Community Colleges Series* (Vol. 136). San Francisco: Jossey-Bass.

Mellow, G. O., & Heelan, C. M. (2008). *Minding the dream: The process and practice of the American community college.* Lanham, MD: Rowman & Littlefield.

Miller, R., & Chandra, S. (2015, June). No respect: U.S. recovery might wind up becoming longest ever. *Bloomberg Business.* Retrieved from http://www.bloomberg.com

Mitchell, M., & Leachman, M. (2015). *Years of cuts threaten to put college out of reach for more students.* Washington DC: Center on Budget and Policy Priorities. Retrieved from http://www.cbpp.org/research/state-budget-and-tax/years-of-cuts-threaten-to-put-college-out-of-reach-for-more-students

Mullendore, R. H., & Banahan, L. A. (2005). Designing orientation programs. In M. Upcraft, N. Gardner, & B. Barefoot (Eds.),

Challenging and supporting the first-year student (pp. 391–409). San Francisco, CA: Jossey-Bass.

Mullin, C. M. (2010). *Doing more with less: The inequitable funding of community colleges.* (Policy Brief 2010-03PBL). Washington, DC: American Association of Community Colleges.

Mullin, C. M. (2012, February). Why access matters: The community college student body. (Policy Brief 2012-01PBL). Washington, DC: American Association of Community Colleges.

Palmer, J. (1986). Bolstering the community college transfer function. Los Angeles: ERIC. Retrieved from http://files.eric.ed.gov/fulltext/ED276492.pdf

Parnell, D. (1985). *The neglected majority.* Washington DC: Community College Press.

Pearch, W. J., & Marutz, L. (2005). Retention of adjunct faculty in community colleges. *The Community College Enterprise,* Spring, 29–44.

Perez, T. E. (2014, September). Community colleges: The secret sauce. [Web log post]. Retrieved from https://www.whitehouse.gov

Phelan, D. (2014). The clear and present funding crisis at community colleges. *New Directions for Community Colleges,* 168, 5–16.

Picus, L. O. (1991). Cadillacs or Chevrolets? The effect of state control on school finance in California. Retrieved from http://files.eric.ed.gov

Pincus, F. (1986). Vocational education: More broken promises. In L.S. Zwerling (Ed.), *New Directions for Community Colleges* Series (Vol. 54) (pp. 41–52). Los Angeles: ERIC. Retrieved from http://files.eric.ed.gov

President's Commission on Higher Education. (1947). *Higher education for American democracy: A report.* (6 vols). Washington, DC: U.S Government Printing Office.

Ratcliff, J. L. (1987). "First" public junior colleges in an age of reform. *The Journal of Higher Education,* (58)2, 151–80.

Ratcliff, J. L. (1994). Seven streams in the historical development of the modern American community college. In G.A. Baker III (Ed.), *A handbook on the community college in America* (pp. 3–16). Westport, CT: Greenwood Press.

Reed, M. (2013). *Confessions of a community college administrator*. San Francisco: Jossey-Bass.

Robbins, S. B., Le, H., Davis, D., Lauver, K., Langley, R., & Carlstrom, A. (2004). Do psychosocial and study skill factors predict college outcomes?: A meta-analysis. *Psychological Bulletin*, 130(2), 261–288.

Safran, S., & Visher, M. (2010). *Case studies of three community colleges: The policy and practice of assessing and placing students in developmental education courses*. (NCPR Working Paper). New York: Columbia University, Teachers College, National Center for Postsecondary Research.

Scott-Clayton, J. Crosta, P., & Belfield, C. (2014). Improving the targeting of treatment: Evidence from college remediation. *Educational Evaluation and Policy Analysis*, 36(3), doi: 10.3102/0162373713517935

Scrivener, S., Weiss, M. J., Ratledge, A., Rudd, T., Sommo, C., & Fresques, H. (2015). *Doubling graduation rates: Three-year effects of CUNY'S Accelerated Study in Associate Programs (ASAP) for developmental education students*. MDRC. Retrieved from http://www.mdrc.org

Shaughnessy, M. (1977). *Errors and expectations: A guide for the teacher of basic writing*. New York: Oxford University Press.

Smelser, N., & Schudson, M. (2004). *Proposal for a commission on general education in the twenty-first century*. Berkeley, CA: University of California, Center for Studies in Higher Education.

Snyder, T. D., & Dillow, S. A. (Eds.). (1993). *120 years of American education: A statistical portrait*. Washington, DC: U.S. Department of Education, Office of Educational Research and Improvement, National Center for Educational Statistics. Retrieved from http://nces.ed.gov

Sowers, N., & Yamada, H. (2011). *Pathways impact report*. Stanford, CA: Carnegie Foundation for the Advancement of Teaching.

Sparks, D., & Malkus, N. (2013, January). First-year undergraduate remedial coursetaking: 1999–2000, 2003–04, 2007–08. *Statistics in Brief* (NCES 2013-013). Washington, DC: National Center for Education Statistics. Retrieved from http://nces.ed.gov

Strong American Schools. (2008). *Diploma to nowhere*. Washington, DC: Broad Education. Retrieved from http://www.broadeducation.org

Tappen, H. (1969). *American education: Its men, ideas and institutions*. New York: Arno Press.

The College Board. (2013). Trends in college pricing. *Trends in Higher Education Series*. Retrieved from http://trends.collegeboard.org/sites/default/files/college-pricing-2013-full-report.pdf

Thelin, J. R. (2011). *A history of American higher education*. (2nd ed.). Baltimore: The Johns Hopkins Press.

Thernstrom, S. (1980). *Progress and poverty: Social mobility in a nineteenth century city*. Cambridge, MA: Harvard University Press.

Tollefson, T. A. (1994). The evolution of state systems of community colleges in the United States. In G. A. Baker III (Ed.), *A handbook on the community college in America: Its history, mission, and management* (pp. 74–81). Westport, CT: Greenwood Press.

Townsend, B. K., & Dougherty, K. (Eds.). (2006). Community college missions in the 21st century. *New Directions for Community Colleges Series* (Vol. 136). San Francisco: Jossey-Bass.

Tyson, C. (2014, July). For community colleges, post-recession blues. *Inside Higher Ed*. Retrieved from https://www.insidehighered.com

U.S. Department of Veterans Affairs. (2013). History and timeline. *Education and training*. Washington, DC. Retrieved from http://www.benefits.va.gov/gibill/history.asp

U.S. Department of Education. (2014). Table 326.20: Graduation rate from first institution attended within 150 percent of normal time for first-time, full-time degree/certificate-seeking students at 2-year postsecondary institutions, by race/ethnicity, sex, and control of institution: Selected cohort entry years, 2000 through 2010. National Center for Education Statistics. Retrieved from http://nces.ed.gov

U.S. Department of Education. (2014). Table 326.30. Retention of first-time degree-seeking undergraduates at degree-granting postsecondary institutions, by attendance status, level and control of institution, and percentage of applications accepted: 2006 to 2013. National Center for Education Statistics. Retrieved from http://nces.ed.gov

U.S. President's Commission on Higher Education. (1947). *Higher education for American democracy.* (Vols. 1–6). Washington, DC: Government Printing Office. Retrieved from http://babel.hathitrust.org/cgi/pt?id=coo.31924013013606

Vaughan, G. B. (1986). *The community college in America: A short history.* Washington, DC: American Association of Community and Junior Colleges.

Vaughan, G. B. (2006). *The story of community colleges.* Washington, DC: American Association of Community Colleges.

Veysey, L. (1965). *The emergence of the American university.* Chicago: The University of Chicago Press.

Visher, M. G., Weiss, M. J., Weissman, E., Rudd, T., & Wathington, H. D. (2012, July). *The effects of learning communities for students in developmental education: A synthesis of findings from six community colleges.* New York: Columbia University, Teachers College, Community College Research Center, National Center for Postsecondary Research. Retrieved from http://files.eric.ed.gov

Wachen, J., Jenkins, D., & Van Noy, M. (2011). How I-BEST works: Findings from a field study of Washington State's Integrated Basic Education and Skills Training Program. *Community College Review, 39*(2), 136–159. doi: 10.1177/0091552111406108

Wilson, R. (1986). Minority students and the community college. In L. S. Zwerling (Ed.), *New Directions for Community Colleges, 54,* 61–70. Los Angeles: ERIC. Retrieved from http://files.eric.ed.gov

Witt, A. A., Wattenbarger J. L., Gollattscheck, J. F., & Suppiger, J. E. (1994). *America's community colleges: The first century.* Washington, DC: American Association of Community Colleges.

Wyner, J. S. (2014). *What excellent community colleges do: Preparing all students for success.* Cambridge, MA: Harvard Education Press.

Zumeta, W. (2011). The great recession: Implications for higher education. *The NEA 2010 Almanac of Higher Education,* 29–42. Washington, DC: National Education Association.

Zwerling, L. S. (1986). Lifelong learning: A new form of tracking. In L. S. Zwerling (Ed.), *New Directions for Community Colleges, 54,* 53–60. Los Angeles: ERIC. Retrieved from ERIC http://files.eric.ed.gov

About the Author

EDUARDO MARTÍ, served as *interim* President of Bronx Community College and as Vice Chancellor for Community Colleges of the City University of New York, and is president *emeritus* Queensborough Community College. Prior to his experience in NYC, he served as President of Corning Community College of the State University of New York (SUNY), and as President of SUNY's Tompkins Cortland Community College. Dr. Martí also served as Executive Dean of Tunxis Community College (Campus CEO, CAO) and Acting President of Middlesex Community College, both located in Connecticut.

An advocate for high standards and the traditional values of education, Dr. Martí serves on the Board of Trustees of Teachers College at Columbia University, as a member of the Board of Governors of the Council for Aid to Education, and as a member of the Board of Directors of Gateway to College. Previously, he served as a member of NYS Governor's Commission on Educational Reform, and on The College Board's Advisory Board on Community Colleges as well as the Community College Research Center Advisory Board of Teachers College at Columbia University. Additionally, he served as Chair of the Board for the Hispanic Educational Telecommunications System (HETS).

Having previously served on the Board of the American Association of Community Colleges (AACC), he was elected once again in March 2009–11. He was elected as a member of the Middle States Commission on Higher Education in October 2010. In 2011 he was appointed by Mayor Bloomberg to serve on the Panel for Educational Policy of the NYC Department of Education.

Three times a graduate of New York University, Dr. Martí holds the Bachelor of Arts, Master of Science, and Ph.D. degrees in biology from the institution. He is the recipient of the Founders Day Award from New York University and was chosen as the recipient of the New York University Alumni Association's *Distinguished Alumnus Award* in November 2007. In October 2008, the *New York Post* honored Dr. Martí with their *Liberty Medal Award* as a champion of human rights. He was previously named to the Honor Roll of Phi Theta Kappa, the international honor society for two-year colleges.

As the recipient of a Fulbright-Hays Seminars Abroad award, he spent June 2004 traveling in China with leaders of minority-serving institutions.

Dr. Marti retired to Cape Cod and lives with his wife Patricia. He has three grown children, Julie, Emily, and Jason, and three grandchildren, Jelani, Laila and Ruby. The birth of the fourth grandchild, Rose, is anticipated in the Spring, 2016.

Index

ABOUT HUDSON WHITMAN

Hudson Whitman is a small press affiliated with Excelsior College, which has its administrative offices in Albany, New York.

Our tagline is "Books That Make a Difference" and we strive to publish high-quality nonfiction books and multimedia projects in areas that complement Excelsior's interest in health, military, and alternative higher education.

If you would like to submit a manuscript or proposal, please feel free to review the guidelines on our website, www.hudsonwhitman.com. We will respond within 6–8 weeks.

OTHER TITLES BY HUDSON WHITMAN

Lightning Source UK Ltd.
Milton Keynes UK
UKOW02f2319131216
289931UK00001B/33/P